Married Priests & Married Nuns

Edited and with an Introduction by
James F. Colaianni

Married Priests
&
Married Nuns

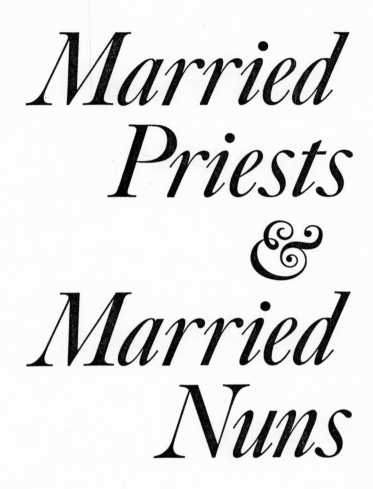

 a Ramparts book

McGraw-Hill Book Company · *New York* · *Toronto* · *London* · *Sydney*

To my wife

Contents

Introduction

James F. Colaianni

The "purity paddle" still exists in some Italian Catholic seminaries. This ancient utilitarian device—a small, wooden oar—is issued to young seminarians, complete with instructions. The student quickly learns how to employ the paddle to tuck in his shirt while maintaining the maximum possible distance between his hand and his genitals. It would be difficult to find a more apt illustration of the results of the five-century-long Latin Scholastic domination of Catholic moral teaching.

The Council of Trent (1545–1568) piously anathematized anyone who "says that the marriage state is to be preferred to the state of virginity or of celibacy and that it is not better and holier to remain in virginity or celibacy than to be joined in marriage." This vocational hierarchy of values rested on a one-sided extrapolation of Pauline texts by a long list of Church Fathers and Doctors (so titled for their "eminent learning and high degree of sanctity"), each of whom seemed to aspire to pre-eminence in the expression of low regard for women. A woman was "a sicked she-ass" . . . "the advance post of hell" . . . "a desirable calamity" . . . "a necessary evil." (Even now Church authority betrays a strong reluctance to give up a theology of sex which relegates women to the status of utilitarian baby machines.) Moreover, the development of the doctrine of Original Sin was compatible with a Manichaean emphasis on sexual union as basically evil. Although the demands of "a weak-

ened nature" were conceded, and marital intercourse, therefore, was not sinful, nevertheless the line between tolerance
and condemnation was often finely drawn. But there was
always the dictum of Genesis—"increase and multiply"—to
keep the black spots from outnumbering the white spots and,
as St. Thomas Aquinas seemed to imply, somebody had to
do the dirty work.

But if it is true that the purity-paddle mentality has been
the dominant strain running through the entire course of
Catholic teaching, it is also true that there have been other
voices. With some justification, Paul Blanshard asserts, "St.
Paul was deeply prejudiced against women, and if he was ever
married, it must have been unhappily." (*Paul Blanshard
on Vatican II.* Beacon Press.) But in citing several of the
well-known Pauline texts which strongly support this contention, Blanshard's own deep-rooted prejudice against
celibacy moves him to ignore the other Pauline texts which
point toward a marked ambivalence in St. Paul's thinking:
"A bishop then, must be blameless, married but once . . .
keeping his children under control and perfectly respectful"
(I Tim. 3:1–4); "Deacons should be men who have been
married but once, ruling well their children . . ." (I Tim.
3:12); "Husbands, love your wives, just as Christ also loved
the Church and delivered Himself up for her . . . that He
might present it to Himself the Church in all her glory, not
having spot or wrinkle or any such thing, but that she
might be holy and without blemish. Even thus ought husbands to love their wives as their own bodies. He who loves
his wife, loves himself. For no man ever hated his own flesh;
on the contrary he nourishes it and cherishes it . . . let
each one of you also love his wife just as he loves himself"
(Eph. 5:25–33). The irony of the situation cannot be missed:
a professional anti-Catholic and the Catholic hierarchy both
playing the game of anti-contextual exegesis, one in the defense of celibacy, the other in its condemnation—both

appealing to the same source. Contemporary Scripture scholarship rightfully deplores such self-serving "use" of the Bible.

Through ecclesiastical discipline Catholics have, down the centuries, amply reflected the chaotic, ambivalent Pauline doctrine. To quote Voltaire:

> The first Christians did not consider celibacy a virtue. Nearly all the apostles and disciples were married. St. Paul wrote to Titus, "Choose for a priest him who is the husband of one wife, having believing children, and not under accusation of dissoluteness." The proceedings of the Council of Nicaea on the subject of married priests deserve attention. Some bishops proposed that priests thenceforward put away their wives, but St. Paphnucius the Martyr strenuously opposed it, observing that marriage was chastity; and the bishops of the Council adopted his opinion.
>
> After that time celibacy was recommended to the clergy without being commanded. Saint Jerome, a devout recluse, was, of all the Fathers, highest in his eulogiums of celibacy in priests, yet he resolutely supported the cause of Carterius, a Spanish bishop who had been married twice. "Were I to enumerate," said he, "all the bishops who have entered into second nuptials, I should name as many as were present at the Council of Rimini."
>
> At length, after several councils on the subject of celibacy had been held without effect, Pope Gregory excommunicated all married priests, either to add respectability to the Church by its greater rigor, or to attach more closely by Rome the priests of other countries, who thus have no other family than the Church. (Voltaire's *Alphabet of Wit*. Peter Pauper Press)

Married men may be ordained to the priesthood in the Catholic Eastern rites; in the Western rites this practice is outlawed and, further, the ordinary lot of the priest who marries is excommunication. Although official statistics on the growing number of defecting priests in the Western Church usually are not released by the bishops, it is now well known that the problem—due in the main to the celibacy rule—has become enormous. Most informed sources are agreed that they total in the tens of thousands. The lowest estimate I have seen for the United States alone is 4,000, the highest, 15,000.

Moreover, seminary dropouts are reaching new highs; and seminary enrollment is down. Bishops throughout the country are privately expressing their deep concern over the prospect of an early, acute "priest shortage," certain to develop in the absence of an early solution.

The "debate" has reached a level of intensity higher, perhaps, than the Catholic birth-control controversy. Indeed, it is not difficult to see that there is some direct relationship between these issues. Father Peter Riga suggests that in his essay. The advocates of change in the Church's traditional teaching on artificial contraception have placed heavy emphasis on the broadest dimensions of the marriage relationship, as an entire human relationship of whole persons and not merely as an exercise in prudential intercourse. Many a young priest coming to an understanding of marriage in this "new light" thus feels betrayed. Whereas formerly he could be taught to think of "wife and family" as "distraction" properly avoided, now—principally as the result of the Church's theological re-examination of marriage prompted by the birth-control issue—he sees new possibilities for true human fulfillment never before revealed to him. His seminary courses on marriage were conducted largely by moral theologians who ignored the 1,500-year history of the Church before the Council of Trent.

Because Trent said that celibacy is "more blessed and better than marriage," the seminarian was conditioned to regard it as liberating—"the best of all states in which to serve the Church." Yet for centuries a married priesthood was understood to be compatible with the Church's mission —and socially acceptable. Moreover, for hundreds of years the obligation to "marry in the Church" applied only to the marriage of a priest. Now that the whole concept of priestly celibacy is being seriously and publicly called into question by Catholics, there are many married priests anxious to abandon an earlier reticence and desire for anonymity. They wish to make a positive contribution toward a more fruitful debate by publicly revealing the personal experiences and attendant insights that are uniquely theirs.

A man shows great courage who will follow his conscience and his love for a woman in spite of threats and prospects of ecclesiastical excommunication, social ostracism, maternal hysteria, and family disownment. (This treatment often extends also to the wife of an ex-priest.)

It is the purpose of this book to provide a specially selected cross-section of forthright clerical opinion on the question. The contributors represent a wide range of background and experience, ranging from an English archbishop to a priest-missionary in Peru. Included are the personal experiences of several married priests who frankly discuss some of the conditions of their withdrawal, as well as the inequity of their present status as they see it. As one of them has said:

> We are all, or nearly all, men of at least average intelligence and more than average education. We are not freaks of nature, nor devils incarnate, nor are we, as we are sometimes embarrassingly regarded, heroes. . . . I do not know how their stories will end. I do not know how mine will end. I only know that God is wherever we are . . . and the battered heart brought low He will not spurn.

In addition, this book includes a candid treatment of other causes of the serious priest-shortage that threatens the Church: inadequacies in seminary education, extreme author-

itarianism on all levels of the clerical ladder, tyrannical sup-
pression of efforts by socially aware priests to relate their
religion to the concrete order, lack of lines of communication between lower clergy and the hierarchy, absence of
grievance procedures, summary disciplinary action with no
right of appeal, and the like.

It is evident that the Church is beset with similar problems in recruiting candidates to the convent life. The drop-
out rate among nuns is progressively rising.

Since Pope John's call for an updated Church, participa-
tion in the process of "creeping intellectual freedom" has,
in general, been more intense in the sisterhood than in the
priesthood. Thus a nun speaks of

> . . . the great difficulty of renouncing [sex] without pay-
> ing the price of neurotic isolation. . . . To arrive at real
> freedom to choose it is necessary to have experienced
> more than superficially the adult world . . . the likely
> costs of the sexual renunciation . . . our usual "recruit-
> ment" policies and programs of "formation" begin to ap-
> pear incredibly naive. . . . A young girl, barely graduated
> from high school, is placed in a restrictive, protective en-
> vironment, one where her associations with men are few
> and codified, where her economic needs are met as ma-
> ternally as any young child's in a middle-class family, and
> where, above all, her opportunities to experience directly
> a wide range of attitudes, values, and life styles are mini-
> mal, this girl notably lacks the experiential conditions to
> choose sexual renunciation. Her "education to reality" is
> a study in naivete.

Although a married sisterhood would hardly be compatible
with the existing convent system, the question is raised:
Why not construct a new, parallel, marriage-oriented ministry for nuns? Thus, women who desire careers in the service of the Church would have an option with respect to
celibacy. In the ideal situation, priest and nun could be

husband and wife. This intriguing notion is dealt with by two of the book's contributors.

Pope Paul VI has shown by his cavalier treatment of a majority of the Church's bishops who seemed eager to place the question of celibacy on the agenda at Vatican Council II (See the Bunnik article) and by statements he has released subsequently, most notably in his encyclical *Sacerdotalis Caelibatus*, that he is unwilling to lead an open reappraisal of this "delicate" subject—too "delicate," he said, for bishops to handle. But this is only to compound the issue. Like artificial contraception it is simply too hot to handle in the traditional "father knows best" style. And it is highly probable that the debate will intensify rather than diminish, notwithstanding the impatient tone of the encyclical and the demand for a "loyalty" of silence made by the American bishops at their national meeting in Washington, D.C., November, 1967. "It is clear," said the bishops in a formal statement, "that an encyclical is not necessarily infallible teaching. It is, however, an exercise of the responsibility of the Holy Father to teach, guide, and unify the Church. As such, it calls for religious assent. With sorrow we say that some voices we hear today can hardly be described as expressing respectful acceptance. Let those who speak in such manner realize that they give the impression of not only challenging established discipline but of rejecting values that touch our Catholic beliefs to the scandal of the faithful and with notable detriment to vocations." Moreover, it is likely that, as with most important solutions of serious problems of morality and discipline in the Church to date, positive action will be generated from below.* Per-

* A case in point is the formation, in February, 1966, of the National Association for Pastoral Renewal, an independent organization of priests concerned with celibacy and other priestly problems. The group has conducted a number of surveys which indicate a high degree of grass roots priest support of its proposal to create a self-supporting, married, ordained ministry.

haps, in the long run, this is the best course to follow. It seems to be the only sure method of bringing to bear the creative ideas of all members of the Church on important issues.

The Second Vatican Council's document on the Church, *De Ecclesia,* has been hailed by avant-garde theologian Gregory Baum as "the basic charter for the reform of the Church in our century." It contains a provision which could develop into a major breakthrough in the struggle to reform celibacy legislation. *De Ecclesia* provides for a married diaconate (deacons are one order below a fully-ordained priest) under certain conditions. It is the editor's hope that this book will be a contribution toward earnest official consideration of an early extension of this attitude to the priesthood and the sisterhood.

Whoso would be a man, must be a nonconformist. He who gathers mortal palms must not be hindered by the name of goodness, but must explore if it be goodness. Nothing is at last sacred but the integrity of your own mind. Absolve you to yourself, and you shall have the suffrage of the world.

EMERSON

A Good Young Priest

Cornelius Outcault

CORNELIUS OUTCAULT is thirty-four, a New Yorker, and a married priest. He was ordained in 1959. From May, 1959, to June, 1962, Father Outcault was a parish priest at Our Lady of Miraculous Medal Church in Long Island. From 1962 to June, 1966, he worked in the same capacity at St. Ignatius Martyr parish in Long Beach (New York). His last priestly assignment came in June, 1966, as a student counselor at Maria Regina High School in Uniondale (New York). The following month his marriage ceremony in Elkton (Maryland) was performed by an Episcopal priest. Several weeks later he resigned from his school post and from his priestly ministry. He is now employed by a New York City stock brokerage firm. Mr. and Mrs. Outcault live on Long Island.

The sun was up. Twelve hours had passed since I had made my decision to leave the priesthood. Where to go, what to do for a living, how to break the news to family and friends were the questions that kept me awake for hours. I offered my last Mass and retired to my rooms, there to write a letter of resignation to the principal of the high school where I taught. The deed was done. I sat for about five minutes, thinking. It was time to leave. Butterflies in my stomach, I walked, a bit relieved, to my car. When I closed the car door and drove away, it was like closing a door on everything. I felt very, very alone. And I was, except for my wife. After seven years, my priesthood was ended. And I was moving into a new life of my own choosing. So much that had become before had been prefabricated and handed to me.

I had previously believed that I could live apart from my wife for a whole year, until a psychiatrist counseled me to the contrary. Sneaking around making love and then separating for days at a time just would not do, and I quickly abandoned the plan to hide the fact of marriage and remain in my job at the school for a year.

It was also pointed out to me that many of the youngsters in school who would come to me for advice would become involved in my world and I in theirs. What effect would my leaving have on a group of fourteen- and fifteen-year-old boys and girls? My wife didn't try to talk me into leaving,

3

but when I called her on the afternoon of my decision she was ecstatic.

How does a man who went through Catholic grammar school, high school, college, and seminary, and who has been ordained disregard so much of everything he was taught? How can a man forsake the priesthood when he knows that so many people he loves hold it in such high esteem? Is the reason just a woman or is it a whole new way of looking at life?

I had read Mortimer Adler's charge that Catholics are so impressed by their possession of "all the truth" that they have no need to look outside themselves for any of it, and it hit home. A Catholic seminary can have a hypnotic effect; a seminarian feels he is equipped with every answer to every human problem that might come up in the course of his ministry. Yet, he has seen so little of life, he cannot possibly begin to imagine what it is all about. Nevertheless, he is led to believe that he is fully equipped as a judge, counselor, and confidant to all comers. Fortunately some priests, at least, mature early enough to come to grips with their lack of experience and knowledge; for others it is a painful, uphill, never-ending struggle—often leading to disastrous consequences.

Of all the people (my wife excluded) who influenced my decision to leave the priesthood, one in particular stands out. I met him two years after my ordination. He had been ordained at least ten years before me, was an accomplished Scripture man, and an intelligent, sympathetic person. He was perceptive to an uncanny degree, a quality that endeared him to many. He was also an avid reader and helped me to get the best out of my own reading program. His interests were varied, more so than those of any other priest I have known.

This person became, in a sense, my tutor. Because of him New York City was no longer the horrible and threatening place I had imagined. We began to see some of the better plays on Broadway. We talked endlessly about all sorts of probems and challenges that faced both us and the Church. I could talk for hours with him and still hope the conversation would never end. It was a brand new education and more satisyfing than any other I had had. Here was a very real person, not made in the mold of so many religious images, but someone who appreciated himself and others as persons. His favorite saying was "To thine own self be true." It never seemed trite; it added a new dimension to my life.

I was deeply moved when my friend decided to trust me with his most intimate secret: He was a homosexual. His admission helped me to begin seeing people for the first time in my life. My casual response gave me a sense of newfound maturity, and he seemed relieved at my reaction. Suddenly I was able to comprehend something of the real loneliness of another human being: He had been in anguish over his secret for ten years, unable to find a single person he could trust to be sympathetic—a terrible indictment of the cold, impersonal, dehumanizing style of life into which his priesthood had propelled him. There was nothing sick or perverted in our new relationship, only a companionship that tried to fathom our common longings. We respected each other's personality and conscience. I could only blame myself and the whole system that mangled and tortured a human being this way. How irrational is this powerful force that touches so deeply the lives of so many individuals!

When I was ordained I was, no doubt, an adequate stereotype of the "good young priest." I followed the book. I spent days off at "days of recollection," there to hear the ground rules for all good priests re-emphasized again and again. I always felt good leaving those spiritual tune-ups, determined to try harder.

In the parish, I did my appointed work, said all my

prayers, and whenever I missed any, I automatically entertained orthodox guilt-feelings over my submission to "laziness." I was always running into Church to "make visits"; I tried to be on time for everything, especially meals in the rectory. The parish wasn't shaken by my presence, but I did cut a mean figure as a "good" priest. I felt very comfortable, very holy, very saved. But something was wrong; something was missing. I felt frustrated, unproductive, uncreative—contributing to nothing.

I kept turning over and over in my mind a few lines from *Cure of Mind and Cure of Soul* by Dr. Goldbrunner, a priest-psychiatrist: "Professional life compels the soul to put on a uniform. . . . There is a danger that the teacher (or priest) may identify himself with his role and become incapable of separating himself from it. He no longer knows he is playing a role and always wearing a mask in front of his spiritual face. . . . He identifies himself with it. His character fails to develop in the round, it gets set in a groove." This is what I feared was happening to me. Never to be yourself, only what the rules and the "good" people around you wanted you to be. I began to fight back. Slowly but resolutely I effected attitude changes, dismissing old fears.

For example, I no longer allowed people around me to intimidate me by blacklisting certain friends they did not like or by scolding me like a child. I was grateful for the lesson I had learned from Goldbrunner: "Before it has a chance of expressing its own view, the soul has an attitude forced upon it. It has no chance of trying out its own feeling. . . . The most valuable and intimate thing in man— the person, which has capacity to make its own decisions—is asleep."

It was becoming clearer—the importance that I held as a person to others as persons, not merely as a "man of the cloth." I felt more and more the desire to understand, and doffing my clerical garb seemed the only way. In social work, the good case worker strives to be "nonjudgmental" with clients, and the collar seemed to be judging all the time. People really aren't themselves when confronted with priests. They are therefore afraid and reluctant to speak when they should speak. Often they merely say, "Oh, but you wouldn't understand," to a man who is supposed to be the epitome of understanding. They have experienced so much lack of empathy with their problems that they are fearful and hardened. They are not treated as people but as cases out of a morals book. Catholics are sick and tired of being berated in sermons, tongue-lashed in confessionals, and having the book thrown at them in rectory parlors. I think it is fair to say that the traditional, Catholic, five-century-old idea of a priest is now obsolete, even funny. Most Catholics are either amused or fed up.

In 1964—I had been a priest for five years—a young girl called the rectory where I was stationed and made an appointment with me for "counseling." I saw her at the rectory that evening. After more than an hour's small-talk I realized that she had no particular problem; she was flirting with me. I felt smitten, but I managed to convey a proper, priestly indignation, as I admonished her not to come back. The tone of her insistence on a second appointment suggested that my vulnerability was being tested. I finally gave in and the following week we re-enacted the performance of our first meeting. This time I was firm and I didn't hear from Linda again until six months later when I received a book she had mailed to me—a Christmas present. Except for my polite thank-you note there was no further communication between us until March when she roared up to the rectory on her motorcycle. Her offer to take me for a ride excited me. Quickly I doffed my cassock and as I settled onto the back of the bike I could feel her whole body trembling. We rode around the block, kidded a little, and then, as I watched her puttering away, I wondered if I would ever see her again. Some weeks later she showed up again, coyly announcing that she had no place to keep her motorcycle. Could she keep it in the rectory garage? It was the beginning of our clandestine courtship.

We would tuck ourselves away in little corners of Jones Beach or meet in Manhattan, always avoiding places where we would be likely to run into parishioners. It was not long before we began to think about marriage. (I had already been thinking abut leaving the priesthood.)

One day at the beach—it was July, 1966—we decided to get married. We chose the first day of Linda's vacation, and so on Monday, July 25, we drove into Elkton, Maryland. We were both a little scared, and incredibly naive. Overwhelmed by all the tinseled "marryin' Sam" places we couldn't decide where to stop. We wondered what to do, what would be the first step. Finally we went into one of the chapels and were both simultaneously repelled by the aura of gross commercialism. We quickly left.

We decided to look up either a Presbyterian or an Episcopal minister in order to insure a more "religious" atmosphere. We found a friendly Episcopalian who seemed sincerely interested in us. He advised us not to "race into this thing" and we agreed to his suggestion of a three-day waiting period (during which time he gave us marriage instructions). Following the ceremony on Thursday we returned to Long Island almost at once. Because we had agreed to keep our little secret from all but a few trusted close friends until I was ready to resign from the priesthood, I dutifully delivered my bride to her home and grudgingly retired to the rectory. Our wedding night was a bust. The following night we managed to celebrate our honeymoon after dining with two of our "trusted" friends. A few days later I was transferred seventy-five miles from Linda's home. It took another five weeks for me to screw up enough courage to resign. During this time I continued to say Mass and perform other duties of the ministry. The fact that I had broken Canon Law did not bother me at all. There was no guilt complex. I still took my Mass seriously, but as for my other duties, I felt that I was just going through the motions. I had no stomach at all for teaching catechism to converts; it was difficult—and dishonest, I suppose—to follow the book on such things as indulgences, in which I no longer believed. In the confessional I merely listened, pronounced the words of absolution and sent the penitents on their way.

There was no eye-to-eye confrontation with Church authorities when I left. I simply dispatched a note to my immediate superior and walked out. Also, by letter, I advised the bishop I was leaving but did not acquaint him with my current marital status. Two months later I sent him a long letter, spelling things out in detail. To this date he has not acknowledged either letter.

Linda's parents, both Catholic, were no problem. They had been aware of our seeing each other and had tried to counsel Linda against "getting involved with a priest . . . priests have lots of problems . . . they fall easily," etc. Their major concern was that Linda might get very emotionally involved in a dead-end affair. I think they were relieved to learn that we had married.

Some other reactions were: "As far as I'm concerned, you served the people as a good parish priest." (friend and parishioner); "I have not made any judgments, except to believe you are doing what you consider best." (former pastor); "Frankly, my reaction to your news was one of relief rather than shock, since it was evident for a long time that you were facing a difficult dilemma." (friend and parishioner); "You chose to leave for a decidedly difficult way of life and I am certainly not going to banish you from my Christmas card list. I contend that one of the factors of friendship is a certainty that your friends are happy and content." (friend); "The first thing I feel I must say is that my love and admiration for you is still the same and always will be. You are my brother before you were a priest and this is what is important. How you choose to serve God is your own concern." (my sister, a nun); "My only concern now is for you to have happiness. You've made your choice, now live it well—with happiness, contentment, and satisfaction, also with the knowledge that you've made lots of friends and those that really are friends will always be behind you; the others aren't important." (friend); "What you have done is both honest and courageous. I only hope that in making your decision you were certain (as certain as one can be) that you wanted your life to follow a difficult pattern, one which you had carefully thought out. Anyway, you know that you have as much understanding from me as you want and you will be very much in my thoughts throughout this period of readjustment." (friend and priest); "From your letter you seem to be happy with the move which is great." (friend and priest); "I still don't know what to say, but I'm writing in spite of that fact, if for no other reason than to let you know that I do care very much about you and about what happens to you. . . . I am terribly sorry that you had to suffer such painful experiences and to face such painful decisions." (friend and priest); "Just a line to say hello and to let you know that I really care and wish to maintain friendship if you want to." (friend and priest).

The great joy of my life is Linda, of course. Linda is all the nice things, full of warmth and understanding, always conscious of the other's feelings and needs, always doing something for someone—or some animal. Perhaps the finest compliment I can pay her is to say that I know she never thinks of me as an "ex-priest," even though I have never asked her about this.

Someone asked me recently if I would consider "going back," assuming a change in the rules. Perhaps I would, but only if I could maintain my private family life, away from anything like a rectory. I would want to keep my job and work in a parish part time, possibly on weekends, or just Sundays. But never would I consider going back to anything like that drudgery of rectory life—even if I could go home every night. I have long since filled out my last baptismal certificate. Any new ministry for me would have to be based upon the principle of real service to real people. I can no longer genuflect before abstractions.

Meanwhile, I'll be more than happy to remind myself now and then of my seventeen-year-old sister's greeting when she first saw me after I left the priesthood: "Gee, you look good in a suit and tie."

A Holy Alliance

The Background, an Interview,
and Correspondence

Robert and Frances Eder

FRANCES EDER entered the convent at age nineteen. For fifteen years she labored as a teaching nun in the order of the Sisters of Mercy in Brooklyn. Now, as Mrs. Eder, she is engaged in social work in Brooklyn.

ROBERT EDER was a parish priest in Brooklyn for three years until June 27, 1966, when he married Frances in Brooklyn City Hall. He is now a mutual fund salesman.

The Eders reside in Brooklyn.

Robert Eder

In April, 1966, when I went to see my bishop to tell him that I wanted to marry, he thought my spirituality had shriveled up, that my choice indicated a lack of faith and a scorn for the priesthood. I understood his thoughts, because I knew even before talking to him exactly what he would say. The Catholic Church as an institution is still quite unprepared to accept a spirituality of humanism and optimism.

I have always felt myself to be more humanistic than ascetic. That is why in the seminary Teilhard de Chardin appealed to me so much. Nicolas Corte's description of Teilhard's fascination by even the smallest, most insignificant piece of matter struck a sympathetic chord in me, and I was determined not to allow my attitude of optimism and humanism to be reduced or destroyed by opposite forces in the Church.

I suppose right from the very beginning of my ministry, I realized both intellectually and emotionally that celibacy was a denial of Christian humanistic values and, for me, an evisceration of my basic life-attitude and personal spirituality. Before ordination, while I was a deacon, I had been sent to Puerto Rico for an intensive eight-week Spanish language course, followed by two weeks of field work in a mountain parish. There I succeeded to some degree in seeing life in the context of another culture, a different approach to life. My naive patriotism, my limited ecclesiastical outlook, my ingrained presumption of living at the center of the universe, all were jeopardized, thanks to this shattering cultural experience. The following summer, as a priest, I returned to Puerto Rico to finish the course at the Catholic University in Ponce where I became convinced that so many things I had taken for granted as true and immutable and good were not so at all. I decided that even some of my most liberal thoughts were backward and anti-quated, and had to be dispensed with. When it was time to return to the mainland, I knew I was going back to a culture which could see only itself in the world, a culture static and stagnant in its complacency, whether social, economic, patriotic, or ecclesiastical. Not that Puerto Rico is idyllic or paradisiacal. What mattered was that in Puerto Rico I learned there was another way of doing things, and seeing life, another system of values. I enjoyed those long hours in class, hearing and repeating Spanish phrases, when being a priest did not prevent friendships from growing up between myself and the teachers (most of whom were female college students) and with my fellow classmates, mostly nuns.

I had been molded in a tradition that demanded separation and distance, and I looked askance at the priest who would allow anyone to call him by his first name, especially a woman. In such a setting, I was often depressed. It was such foolishness—this sexual apartheid. In my loneliness, I began to wonder whether celibacy was more cultural than doctrinal and, therefore, subject to change. I could not be sure. My field work that second summer took me to another parish near Caguas in the eastern valley region of the island. Here too, I recognized that celibacy was a liability and a drag. Imposed by another world, by another age, on the priest of today, it makes him live in a schizophrenic world. Here he was, going out to the chapels and barrios of his parish every day, returning late at night, living alone. Tired, physically and mentally drained by an arduous ministry, he was forced to support his ideals and zeal on a foreign, unreal, monastic spirituality of loneliness and celibacy. I began to understand that the burden of celibacy—the loneliness—could be an insurmountable barrier to an effective ministry. I was a product of the authoritarian system inherent in the pre-Vatican Council seminary—a total institution in the strict sense. My seminary was guilty of all the defects spelled out in any current indictment of the Tridentine seminary. It was tightly run, geographically separated from civilization, headed by a rector who had supreme power over the seminarian's living habits, speech, study habits, and everything else, private, public, social, or hygienic! Everyone stood in fear of him; no one really liked him. Whenever he spoke to us it was always on matters of obedience, prudence, and authority. Before Christmas one year, he spoke of the lesson we all should learn from the feast. It was not a lesson of love, but one of obedience. He was a genuine legalist, and proud of it. If we wanted to stay in the seminary, we had to be legalists too.

The rector was not alone in his martinet-like views toward us. The spirit of inflexibility permeated the entire faculty. There was no one between pastor and seminarian willing to take a stand when the rector's edicts were manifestly and blatantly unjust. One priest, in particular, grated on me. He epitomized the clerical state. His cassock was immaculate; he always wore French cuffs; he was distant, aloof and cold; he seemed afraid of people; he demanded absolute compliance with the Rule. The seminary was a direct challenge to my Christian humanism. It made light of personalism, and apotheosized rigidity and obedient compliance. I fought against it constantly; not by flouting the rules, but by obeying, and complying, and yielding at every step. I had the notion that I could challenge the system from within by establishing a "good record." I gave the appearance of being completely docile. I was the ideal seminarian. The rector and faculty approved of me; they gave me positions of responsibility. In my last year they named me Deacon of the Seminary, the "big man" among the seminarians. And all the while I hated the inhuman, ugly, and non-Christian system.

In those days the question of celibacy was not a major preoccupation. I had thought about marriage and celibacy the year before receiving the order of subdeacon (considered a major step toward ordination, because the seminarian implicitly promises perpetual celibacy), but I did not then consider that I would ever have any second thoughts about the Church's law. I had been propagandized into believing that celibacy was the something extra, the distinguishing mark for those who were "perfect." Being abstract, noble, superior, and pure, it appealed to my idealism. Seen in this light, celibacy was attractive to me. There was no reason for me to be wary of it. I was not hypersexual. I had never fallen into the habit of masturbation. I could control my thoughts and desires, and since beginning college I had not been out on dates. On the other hand, celibacy was not so attractive that I would ever have chosen it, were it not attached to ordination as a *sine qua non.*

When the English theologian Charles Davis explained why he left the Church, he said that he could no longer be a part of a church which continuously disregarded the rights of those it was pretending to help toward salvation, and that he was getting married because only through marriage could he hope to rebuild his life according to this personalistic philosophy. I believe there is an intimate connection, obversely, between the lack of personalism in the Church and its celebration of celibacy. In my own case, I could not say that I decided to marry only *because* I had felt this severe dehumanization in the life of the Church. Yet, these two things are so closely bound together for me that one goes necessarily with the other.

My first assignment was to a rundown, inner-city parish in the metropolitan New York area. It used to be a parish of lower-middle-class Irish and Italian families. At that time, some ten years ago, its three- and four-story tenements were taken over by Negroes and Puerto Ricans moving in from Manhattan and other parts of the city. The bishop had been thinking about closing down the parish. The money was low, there seemed little hope for improved Sunday collections, and the parish buildings were in need of costly repairs. Then, a year or two before I was assigned there, the bishop changed his mind—I guess because the baptisms began to average twenty-five to thirty a week. The parish took in so many people that, just by force of numbers, it had to stay open.

My pastor was a nice enough man, but trained and fed on the institutional and static. He was not the man for the job. As a person, he was open to all the parishioners, and deep down he was not prejudiced. Yet in the 1964 presidential elections, while he was pastor, he voted for Goldwater. The irony overwhelmed me. Here we were, in a place where poverty was rampant, where the majority of people were on welfare, where the public schools were clearly inferior, where racial bitterness and hopelessness were on the increase, and the pastor voted for Goldwater!

There were two other priests in the parish at that time, one about fifty, and a younger one, about six years my senior, who became a close friend. The older priest was conservative and took the pastor's position on all but a few questions. That meant that the rectory was divided—the pastor and the oldest curate against the other curate and myself. The pastor objected to our "social" sermons. He especially objected to mine, and felt I was imprudent in the things I said regarding Vietnam and the race situation. It came to a point where, one Sunday afternoon, I found on my desk a typewritten message ordering that in the future nothing should be mentioned in any Sunday sermon regarding the following topics: Martin Luther King, integration, segregation, Negro-Puerto Rican relations, education, bussing of Negro children into all-white schools, local school boards, etc. A copy of this same decree had been given to the other two curates.

I had the feeling that the pastor never understood liberty or responsibility. He gave the impression he never trusted me in my work, although I knew he trusted me as a person. It was strange. He wanted to know about all telephone calls. He was so caught up with the mania of the institution that he completely succumbed to it. As a priest, he must have ceded all liberty and human responsibility to his superiors, and now he was demanding that we do the same. In this lies the story of our many misunderstandings and arguments, oftentimes heated.

The point of describing the personality of my pastor is to show that my thoughts on celibacy were tied up with my view of the structures of the Church. This is not to say that in other parishes the situation was exactly the same, or that there were no pastors who did not understand the issue of freedom. But once I saw that the Church really did accept and harbor untenable positions, it became clear that one's thoughts and actions were subject to the control of whoever happened to hold the reins. In fact, I began to see that celibacy helped to induce docility and submission to authority, insofar as it made the priest dependent, really dependent, on the structure itself. Were he to say "no"—disobey, rebel—to whom could he turn? To no one, and he knew it, and the pastor knew it, and the bishop knew it.

In my own case, I became increasingly lonely. I was, in

many ways, a rebel, because, with the younger curate, I fought the party line of noninvolvement in controversial social issues, and I could not endure the dependency the institution expected me to manifest. There were times when I would go up to my room and sit and wish I were married. I wanted to live, not the impersonal life I was living, but a personal one—personal in the sense of dealing with persons and loving them, instead of living and working for an unjust institution which, in the long run, did not give a damn about anyone as long as the money kept coming in. That was the big worry. I saw this, because in taking positions which did not agree with those of higher-ups, I felt the pressure and I understood where the chips were falling. I cannot love people in general, and yet the Church refused to allow me to love them in particular. Why? Perhaps because this would loosen her control on me.

Another thing that bothered me was the way people in the parish regarded my status as a celibate. There were two types of reaction. The first was found in most of the people who came to Sunday Mass regularly. They saw me as a god. I was one who did not need women. For them a quasi-magical halo settled down upon my head. It seemed that all their respect toward me did not come because I was a person, but actually because I was different from the run-of-the-mill. The other reaction came from those who thought it meant that the priest was out of it; that he was out of touch with their lives and with their problems, whether marital or otherwise. Of the two, I found the first to be more offensive. For one thing, the second attitude has some truth to it—an unmarried clergy does miss out on understanding concrete, day-to-day problems. But to honor the celibate because he does not need a woman is to build reverence on a serious misunderstanding of Christian marriage, a misunderstanding which sees it only as a *remedium concupiscentiae* (remedy against unbridled lust). The priest is not married, therefore he is better than we are. This is the implicit reasoning.

In July, 1965—two years after ordination—I met my wife, Fran. The parish had received some $8,000 from Catholic Charities to finance a special summer vacation school and recreation program for the children of the neighborhood. My curate friend and I had been busy recruiting volunteers, mostly nuns, college students, and seminarians, who were free for the summer. Fran was one of the volunteers. At that time she was a nun, teaching first grade at a local parochial school. She was also attending college, and although she had some courses that summer, she came down almost every afternoon to run a storefront located in one of the forgotten corners of our parish.

I was so busy that summer that I hardly knew Fran until about the end of July. The only contact I had with her was when I visited the storefront, to bring the free lunches. I had heard a lot about Fran (Sister Joan) from other sister volunteers. They were surprised I did not know her. She was intelligent, a reader of the new theology, and very radical; also very pretty. Very slim, with deep eyes, she was the only sister I had ever seen who looked at all attractive in her order's grotesque habit.

Frances Eder

Like many others entering a religious community, I had, at age nineteen, great expectations and high morale. I was convinced (at the time) that becoming a nun was the best way possible, or perhaps the only way I then saw possible, of making a total Christian commitment. However, I distinctly remember questioning my decision after about a week in the novitiate. Somehow one week was enough to shake my convictions and to make me wonder if I had not made a mistake after all. It is difficult to put my finger on the exact cause of my disillusionment, but perhaps a few reflections on how things developed for me are in order.

The mistress of novices, the dominant figure in the novitiate, was a cold person, rigid and unbending, and for the most part feared by all. She was completely dedicated to the rules, and any infraction of these rules by unthinking novices or postulants was always taken as a personal affront by her. She ran the novitiate as one would run a total institution. There was no dialogue between the inmates and those in authority. The only thing expected of us was complete docility and obedience. (Once I was told by the mistress to play the piano during the recreation period. Although I replied that I couldn't play without my music she kept insisting that I play. I told her flatly that I was unable to play without music. She was visibly annoyed but said nothing to me then. However, the next day I was corrected for not doing what I was told and for not at least attempting to play.)

Coming from a family background which did not stress obedience excessively and where I was able to speak up and do what I wanted without fear of punishment, I despised the system all the more. However, I decided to stay and take my vows, reasoning that things would be different when I left the novitiate and became actively engaged in teaching or social work.

My first assignment was to teach school in one of our poorer parishes. I was delighted with the prospect of being in touch with people again. (In the novitiate we were not allowed to have any contact with the "outside world" except for an occasional visit from our families.) Although I enjoyed teaching I became, once again, increasingly disillusioned with the life. Renouncing the world and the flesh for the sake of God became at best a very questionable enter-

prise for me, especially when it took the form I so often saw
in nuns I lived and worked with. They somehow spent their
lives despising what should be loved and what should be a
matter of passionate belief.

To tell the truth, many times, even in the first year of the
novitiate, I was on the verge of leaving. The mistress of
novices always told me that I was too proud, too independent. And this was exactly what an old sister said about me
on my first assignment to a Negro parish. She had once
been mistress of novices, and when I arrived fresh from the
novitiate, she assumed, I suppose, that she would deal with
me according to the long-established relationship of absolute superior versus abject inferior. When I showed her that
I was independent and acted on my own, she thought that
my attitude was unbecoming to a sister of our order. To
give an example: once when I was talking to some parishioners outside the church after Sunday Mass, some other
sister reported me, and for two hours she yelled at me, and
thought it matter enough to report to the Mother General.

A year later, I was transferred to a fairly new convent in
a wealthy community on Long Island. Things were about
the same there, only most of the sisters thought themselves
fortunate to be in such a well-off parish. The superior took
great pains to make the convent harmonious with the style
of life of the majority of parishioners. Saturdays were
usually spent arranging and rearranging new art acquisi-
tions. I taught in that school for two years. When I received
my next assignment to an institution for boys, I was happy
to leave the "chic" parish, as I had been involved in a weird
emotional contest between two older sisters who were jealous of each other's friendship with me.

Going to the boys' home seemed to many of the sisters to
be a bad assignment, lacking status and demeaning. For me,
it was one of my most challenging assignments insofar as
there was much work to be done in helping the boys over-

come serious emotional and mental problems that broken homes had caused. It was a chance to relate to these children, not only in a teaching role, but also in a fuller, human way—to be a mother to them, to be their friend, to be with them throughout the day, and to get to know them and love them. Teaching school had not allowed me to know people, even children, in this way. I had always tried to get to know my children well, and often in my first two assignments I had been in trouble for talking to their parents after school, as this practice was, for some inexplicable reason, discouraged. While there, the Mother General scolded me for retaining contacts with the kids I had taught at my previous school, who still wrote to me. She claimed the ideal of the sisters of our order should be not to involve oneself in any sort of contacts with nonreligious people, that is, with anyone outside the convent.

Now that I look back on fifteen years of the warped way of life that was foisted upon me, I see its injustice and meanness. But to me at that time, not knowing any other way except that taught to me in the novitiate, I accepted the system and took it for granted. It is a strange thing, but true, that it is far easier to get into the structure than to get out of it.

My assignment to the boys' school was not always a happy one. I think I would have left within a week of arriving there if I had not distinguished between my work with the boys and my experiences with the superior of the convent and the principal of the school. Both were in their late sixties, and both had bad tempers, bred from a solidly Irish Catholic background. They continuously fought and bickered. I thought then that they were envious of each other's position and authority.

Together with a few other sisters, I became involved with the boys and their activities. I helped the boys set up a Little League baseball team, and arranged games with the more fortunate children who lived in Syosset. This, of course, displeased the superior, as it was once again a sign of my involvement with the outside community, *i.e.,* the world, something dangerous for any sister. She was especially angered and distraught to find that I had even been horseback riding with some of the boys, and asked me how I had been riding, sidesaddle or cowboy fashion! It was at times like these that I packed my suitcase and seriously contemplated walking out the front door and saying, to hell with it! Goodbye!

I continued in this frame of mind, not solidifying my position until the summer of 1964 when I was sent to Puerto Rico to study. Looking back on that summer I realize that I underwent a staggering personal experience. (Some passed it off as a cultural shock, but I knew it was deeper than that.) Putting it simply, I had a glimpse of the real world and my place in it. What this experience had done for me—or to me—was to show itself in the decisions I made and the position I took in terms of my own religious life and the concept of vocation.

I left Puerto Rico determined to face real issues. I suppose I knew these ideas would lead to a direct confrontation with authority and so, when I asked my superiors for the opportunity and time to work with the poor of the diocese, I was not surprised when they told me that this was not our work, that our primary work was education.

It is a sad commentary on religious life that so many of the details of this life are determined by the institutions we own and operate. Thus it becomes a business proposition. We *must* staff and finance our schools, etc., and so we cannot explore other possible structures.

I was finally given permission to work in a poor section for a few hours on Saturday. Accompanying this permission were all kinds of restrictions. Depending more upon my own initiative and personal responsibility than upon conformity to the directions from my superior, I found myself becoming more and more involved with the poor and their problems. I knew that I couldn't long be interested in a religious community that was only interested in itself and not in the world. Because of a lack of exposure to the real world, the community was religiously cozy. There was definitely the need for a new mentality regarding the apostolic life of sisters, and yet any discussion of this topic was sure to be explosive. Customs had often been enforced by recourse to moral pressures and thus, for many, objective evaluation of these practices created varied feelings of guilt and fear.

I suppose I had already chosen between obedience on one hand and fidelity to my new vision of life on the other. I became increasingly alienated from the community with its complex system of customs and laws. Since the very structure of the community life is based upon a medieval attitude toward the world, it stands to reason that what is clearly a semi-monastic structure is not based on a theology which is in and for the world. A sister who is imbued with openness to the world and yet lives within the structure of a quasi-monastic life is bound to be faced with many contradictions.

Editor's Interview with Robert and Frances Eder

ED: Fran, what kind of work were you doing at the store-front?

FRAN: I was doing social work, helping people with their problems and anything else that came along. The people would come to the store for all kinds of assistance. I was taking courses in college in the morning, and then I would work from about 12:30 until maybe 6:00 in the evening.

ED: Did you usually see Bob there?

FRAN: Not often at first, because he was involved in another section of the parish and would just run in and out with messages or instructions. But gradually we developed a real friendship and we began to write letters. It was pretty much like this until January of 1966, then everything changed.

ED: What happened?

FRAN: Well, one night after an almost all-night meeting at the store, Bob was driving me home, and just as I was about to get out of the car he said: "Don't get out; I want to talk to you about something." So I stayed in the car. And then there was a long silence and I was thinking to myself that he probably was going to tell me about something that had happened in the parish—what a hard time the pastor was giving them or something like that—and I waited. It was snowing and I was sitting there, waiting. He was staring straight ahead, not saying anything. Then, finally, after what seemed like an awfully long time, he told me that he loved me. I was afraid. I was shocked. I was confused. I didn't know how to take it.

ED: You didn't expect it?

FRAN: I didn't expect it at all—no. I just sat and didn't say anything. I didn't know what to do. It was at least 5:00 a. m. and I was worried about getting into the convent. I was afraid.

ED: Did anything else happen?

FRAN: You mean after I got back into the convent?

ED: No. Before you left the car.

FRAN: That's a leading question. [*Laughter*] He kissed me. I was in my habit; lots of starchy things and veils, and long rosary beads, and all that, and Bob was wearing his Roman collar. Ordinarily, on a night like that he would be wearing civvys, but there he was—in his priest's suit—and I in my sister's habit. It was quite a scene. When I finally got into the convent it was almost 5:30, time to get up. I just paced up and down my room, waiting for the bell to ring.

ED: Did you think you loved him then?

FRAN: I didn't know. I guess I hadn't thought about it until he brought it up. The next day I was teaching, but I was so distracted I don't really remember being in the class-room.

ED: When did you see Bob again?

FRAN: After school the next day.

ED: Did you talk about what happened the night before?

FRAN: Yes.

BOB: I remember I asked Fran if she was still talking to me, and she answered me that she wasn't angry with me.

ED: How did your relationship proceed from there?

BOB: We saw one another more than we wrote to one another after that, perhaps three nights a week until we were married.

ED: How did you manage to get her out of the convent three nights a week?

FRAN: Well, it was a very large convent. [*Laughter*]

ED: You mean you sneaked out?

FRAN: That's about it—yes.

BOB: She just left through the side gate.

ED: Fran, when did you and Bob begin to talk seriously about getting married?

FRAN: I guess it was in March, wasn't it, Bob?

BOB: Yes.

FRAN: When we finally made up—when I finally made up my mind.

BOB: Well, I wanted to get married and Fran was unsure of herself. And for the first couple of months after that night in January we talked about the problems and difficulties and possibilities of doing it. Many times she would be pessimistic, and other times optimistic. And finally, toward the end of March, we consolidated our ideas and Fran said she definitely did want to get married, and we planned on the end of June.

ED: What were your respective ages then?

FRAN: Bob was twenty-eight; I was thirty-four.

ED: At this time, in March, 1966, was there any inkling in your convent, Fran, that anything was going on?

FRAN: No, not at that time.

ED: When did this first come to the notice of your colleagues?

FRAN: My superior spoke to me at the beginning of May. How long she knew before that, I don't know.

ED: What happened? Do you want to describe that scene?

FRAN: She came to my classroom. I was putting away some books and fixing the classroom, and she said she would like to speak to me for a minute. I was kind of surprised, because she's the major superior of the whole community—not just the superior of that convent—so she was rarely seen around. And she looked kind of upset. She just walked into my room and said: "Are you in love with Father Eder?" And I said: "Yes." And then she just sat down at my desk and didn't say anything for about ten minutes. After that she was upset and she cried a little bit and told me that somebody had told her. She took it very badly. Then she asked me if, before I gave her a definite answer, I would think it over again for another week. She also asked me to take counsel with a local Jesuit. He's a psychologist, well known in the diocese as a counselor of nuns.

ED: What advice did he give you?

FRAN: He told me I should stay in the convent and wait until Bob had legal permission to marry.

ED: From the Church?

FRAN: Yes, legal permission from the Church to marry.

ED: Was this kind of permission available?

FRAN: No.

ED: As I understand it, Canon Law places the priest who wishes to marry in the absurd position of having to break the law before he can seek relief from Rome. That is, he must marry first and suffer automatic excommunication, then file a petition requesting ratification of his act. Is that correct, Fran?

BOB: Yes, but this is no guarantee of favorable action. These proceedings are conducted in such secrecy that no one seems to know the basis upon which decisions are made, the grounds necessary to establish one's case, etc. Canon lawyers in this country are very confused about this. You can never get a straight answer.

ED: Did you point this out to the Jesuit?

FRAN: Yes, I did. He told me that if I left and Bob didn't

have permission, we would never be happy, and God would never bless our marriage.

ED: Do you think he was just trying to stall the whole thing, knowing full well that this kind of permission wasn't available?

FRAN: I don't know. He might have been confused about the mechanics. On the other hand, maybe he was just stalling.

ED: Did you report back to Sister Superior after that?

FRAN: Yes, I reported back. I told her it was good news, but it wasn't the good news she wanted to hear. I told her I definitely wanted to leave the community, and that I was going to marry Bob. I guess she was so upset because she thought I was going to change my mind.

ED: In order to conform to the juridical setup, if you were going to leave the convent and marry you would be required to apply for a dispensation from whatever vows you had already taken?

FRAN: That's right.

ED: And what vows had you taken?

FRAN: I had taken three vows: poverty, chastity, and obedience.

ED: Were these what are commonly called perpetual vows, or were they for a fixed period of time?

FRAN: No, they were perpetual.

ED: Did you make this kind of application?

FRAN: Yes, I did.

ED: And did you get a dispensation?

FRAN: Yes, I did.

ED: In this petition, did you have to reveal the fact that your intended husband was a priest?

FRAN: No, I didn't reveal that. In the formal petition I merely said that I intended to marry. Bob's name did not appear on the petition.

ED: And if it had been required, it would have rendered the whole thing kind of meaningless, right?

FRAN: Yes.

ED: But this is kind of silly, isn't it? I mean, your superior's knowing full well that you intended to leave to marry Bob, and at the same time going through the motions of getting you properly dispensed to leave the convent?

BOB: Well, I had told her I thought even a petition for a dispensation was wrong, because what difference did it make? We didn't give a darn about the law of the Church insofar as Fran marrying an ordained priest was concerned, so why worry about a little thing like formal permission to leave the convent? Even so, I think for Fran it was a question of taking one step at a time; sometimes we aren't ready for another step. A person has to take one step at a time according to his own conscience, and it seems to me for Fran to go ahead just disregarding all the rules would have been completely out of character with her own past. In fact, I petitioned for my own laicization and I regret it now. I certainly knew at the time I would never get it. It was silly, because I knew full well that a remedy was not available. It was silly theologically.

ED: Bob, when did your impending marriage first come to the attention of your pastor?

BOB: The pastor never knew until I was gone. He was a very nervous man. He would shake and frequently blow up, and I thought it would be better not to tell him. I didn't want to upset him.

ED: So you never said anything to him?

BOB: No.

ED: You just packed your bag and left when the time came?

BOB: I had packed my bags three or four weeks beforehand. I told him that I had seen the bishop and the bishop was transferring me.

ED: Had you seen the bishop?

BOB: Yes. I saw the bishop the Saturday after Easter.

ED: When you told him what your intentions were, how did he react?

BOB: He asked me if I had lost my faith. I told him "No," and he said, "Well, I can't believe it. What really do you believe in?" "Well," I said, "I believe that Christ died for us and rose again, and that He loves us." He said, "I really can't believe that you haven't lost your faith. This shows a scorn for the priesthood, and how can you have scorn for the priesthood?" "I feel humanistically inclined," I said, "and I think there is a Christian humanism and marriage has a place in it." And he said to me: "I'll bet you're only saying that to me because of the Second Vatican Council." And I said: "No, it's only because of the Second Vatican Council that I feel that I have freedom enough to come and say this to you face to face." He said to me: "You're the first one who has ever said that." I didn't put much stock in that. He spoke for about an hour and a half. He said to me: "If you're married, don't live in New York City."

ED: Why?

BOB: I surmised because it would be an embarrassment. He thought it would be a scandal. He gave me his blessing. "Well," he said, "I'll pray for you. Kneel down." I knelt down and he gave me his blessing, and I left.

ED: Did he say anything about the fact that Fran was a nun?

BOB: I don't think he knew that she was a nun. I didn't mention it.

ED: And then you went back to your parish?

BOB: That's right.

ED: You continued to function?

BOB: That's right. I told the bishop that I was going to leave at the time of the next appointments.

ED: And he didn't interfere with your going back, or anything like that?

BOB: No.

ED: As far as you know, he didn't tell your pastor?

BOB: No, I don't think so. As far as I know, he didn't.

ED: Did you have any further contact with the Chancery Office?

BOB: I wrote another letter about a month and a half after that. I said: "What I told you, I am going to carry through." Then I received a call from the chancellor. He wanted to see me. I went to his office and he gave me another lecture about why I shouldn't leave, and I was bitched about that. He said we would never be happy. I said: "How do you know, when you've never even met the girl?"

ED: Did he know Fran was a nun?

BOB: Yes, then he knew Fran was a nun. He said we would

never be happy; that she was a nun and I was a priest; that it was against the law; that the fact that she was a nun made her conscience all the more sensitive—so we'd never be happy.

ED: Were there any confrontations with ecclesiastical authorities, other than the one with the bishop and the one with the chancellor?

BOB: No. Well, I let it be known among my friends that I was becoming annoyed at their juvenile attitude toward "saving" me, as it were. . . .

ED: You mean fellow priests?

BOB: Yes.

ED: Did the word get around the parish before you were married?

BOB: No.

ED: Did you take counsel with anyone?

BOB: Yes, I went to a priest friend of mine. I saw him two or three times. At first his attitude was one of surprise, but he listened to me and he talked to me. He dealt with me as a person, and asked me if I was really sure I was in love, and what I meant by love. . . .

ED: What did you mean by love?

BOB: Well, by love I meant a total giving of myself to Fran—material, spiritual, intellectual, emotional, financial. [*Laughter*] He was satisfied. The second time I saw him he said he knew of someone else who was making the move, that he thought I should follow my conscience, and that I shouldn't be daunted by ecclesiastical law if I believed this was my vocation.

ED: What was his status; was he a parish priest?

BOB: A parish priest. He was about forty-five.

ED: Did either your family or Fran's family know about your plans before you got married?

FRAN: Yes, we told my family before, right after I spoke to Mother Superior. Bob said he thought it would be better if we told my sister first. She's married and has three children. She's quite a reader; she reads everything. She has no theological background. She seems quite liberal; she seemed quite liberal on everything up to that point.

ED: How did your sister take it?

FRAN: Well, Bob said that we should tell her first. I didn't know whether we should or shouldn't, but we stopped off there one Saturday after work. She was kind of surprised to see us but thought nothing of it. And then he wanted to tell her and I kind of didn't want him to say anything. But he told her. I was on the phone and he told her and when I came back in the room she was completely shattered, I guess. She was having a drink to calm her nerves. She said she was thinking of our mother and father because they were very orthodox Catholic. And what a shock it would be to them and how terrible it would be because my father was always so proud of my being in the convent and all that. So she was very upset and we were sorry that we told her.

ED: Has your sister since come around? I mean are you on good terms with your sister?

BOB: Yes. Yes. We lived there at first—the whole summer, in fact. We didn't have any place to stay. I'd say we're friends, they want us to forget all about our past. They want Fran to forget she was ever a sister, and I a priest.

FRAN: There's no friction, but they just don't understand

our position at all. Then we went to see my parents. They were very shocked and upset.

BOB: Her father said we were Protestants.

FRAN: I think during those six months before, my mother and father kind of had an inkling. They never approved too much of the kind of work I was doing—different things they'd heard about like being on picket lines. It was a bit too radical for them. Mother always had it in her mind because she told me. She always figured that I wouldn't stay in the convent because one time she said to me, "What would happen if they didn't let you go down there any more; you wouldn't do the things that you wanted to." But they never expected this because they knew Bob. In fact, my mother even sent him a Christmas card and money.

ED: Was there a scene when you told them about it?

FRAN: Kind of a quiet scene, no screaming. My father had a drink. In fact we all had a drink because we could just about take it. And that was it. They expected I was going to leave the convent, but they never expected the double trouble.

ED: Have they since come around?

FRAN: Yes. We are on good terms with them now. We see each other.

BOB: They don't understand.

FRAN: No.

ED: Where did you get married?

BOB: This is an interesting story. We've got to tell it. Because of the hangup, principally a hangup about law, Fran wanted to get married in the Church.

FRAN: A priest friend of Bob's was going to marry us.

BOB: Well, there was a hangup about law: Were we really being faithful to the Church? Were we being good Christians in doing what we were doing? We had decided to get married, but when it came to practice, it was a big stumbling block. At first we thought we would have an ecumenical wedding. We'd have an Episcopal friend of ours marry us. But he chickened out because he decided it was too explosive politically, and for his own reasons, maybe ecumenical, he decided not to. Then we thought we'd have a priest friend of ours marry us but he wisely decided against it, too. He said, "Look, technically, if I were to marry you, that's against Canon Law anyway, and what's the difference if you got married in City Hall, theologically?" So we were kind of at a crisis. Fran didn't want to get married in City Hall. She said she wanted to be married by a priest. It was a very big crisis. This was maybe two days before the wedding. I didn't want to pressure her into doing anything because an individual conscience is an individual conscience, do you know what I mean? Everybody has a whole background of ideas. Anyway, it turned out that we did get married in City Hall on June 27th. Fran's mother and father still think we were married by a priest.

ED: Bob, what about your family?

BOB: My mother and father are both dead. I have one sister married and one sister in a convent. I told my married sister early in February and at first she was shocked, but the next day she called me up and said, "Well, if it's really what you want to do, I think it's a good idea." And she was very positive from that time on.

ED: Is she a Catholic?

BOB: Yes.

ED: What about the nun?

BOB: That's another story with her. She took it just the opposite. She thought it was a bad idea. She hasn't come around about it. She's still kind of bitter about it.

ED: Do you think you made a wise decision?

FRAN AND BOB: Yes! Yes!

ED: Bob, you know there is a lot of heat being generated on this question of celibacy, and it would appear, to some at least, that the day of change may not be too far off. Assuming that sometime in the future the possibility existed for you to re-enter the active ministry as a married priest, would you be interested? Will you be looking forward to that prospect?

BOB: I'm not sure the idea appeals to me at all. And the reason is that I think the whole Church has to change, the whole parish structure, the whole concept of Sunday Mass and collections, and the schools, nuns, clerical status, confession. All of this has to go. What do you think, Fran?

FRAN: I agree.

ED: The only circumstance under which you would be interested in this prospect would be if the basic structure of the institutional Church were to change?

BOB: Yes.

ED: Along the lines being suggested by progressive theologians?

BOB: It has already changed for us.

ED: Yes, but this is a subjective thing. So far as the institutional Church is concerned, you don't exist as a member.

BOB: As far as the juridical institution goes—no. As far as the Church goes—that's another story.

Letters

August 10, 1965
Dear Father,

Decided to write this to you during retreat; therefore only "holy and wholesome" thoughts will be included. The country is so peaceful but somehow I don't feel at home here. For a week, yes. For life, NO. I guess the tempo and rhythm of the storefront neighborhood are too much in my veins. I agree with you that the summer program (in its manifold aspects) has been successful. The possibilities are unlimited; the team approach (including professional, non-professional, lay, and religious) seems to be the most valid one. Looking back over the months, the aspect that I liked best about the storefront was that it was formed with a minimum of preconceived organizational goals and structures, and was intended as an "evolutive institution" to respond to and be formed by "FELT NEEDS." (Don't tell Sr. M. R.— she thinks I'm "way out" because I feel more at home in an unstructured, creative program than in a more formalized one.) Anyway, reading the *Secular City* certainly has confirmed the opinion that the past formulations and structures can't possibly work now. How did I get off on that? . . .

I'm sure I don't have to tell you that I'd love to be involved in the center full time in September. But . . . the possibility of this ever happening is so slim that it doesn't even warrant mentioning. I suppose the price has to be paid in frustration and I guess it's all part of discovering almost immediately the frustrating job of accepting the implications of a human response in Christian love. Anyway, let me know what is happening and what is going to happen in September. Be assured of a remembrance in my prayers; include me in yours,

Sincerely,

S. M. Joan

[ED NOTE: "S. M. Joan" is an abbreviation of Mrs. Eder's name as a nun, "Sister Mary Joan."]

October 25, 1965
Dear Father,

At the risk of being passé I'm writing this to you. I'm thankful for meeting you, for many reasons, but I won't go into them now. However, what really strikes a responsive chord in me is that you admit to knowing only a few of the answers and you ask a lot of the right questions. After talking to you the other night it began to dawn on me that until a person has suffered and questioned why he suffers, he has not yet lived.

The way things are going there isn't much use in my trying to offer answers to your questions. Because, in the first place I have too many questions of my own. However, I've come to realize that the priesthood (or religious life) doesn't operate like a wheel of fortune; when it answers one's questions at all, it does so by suggesting related questions—or by giving hints of explanations that in themselves contain further questions. And so one comes to the frightening realization that the whole picture is terribly greater and more complicated than one had thought.

However, I am convinced (sometimes against my own cowardly will) that the noblest and most sensible way of being in the Church (and in the world) is simply to be a loving man in one's world. There is no good reason in trying to separate these two great realities, and it is just this double sense of things—of God and man—that can burn away the corrosion of selfishness and childishness that assures the majority of us that we can live in the name of God, at a distance from men. I think this is the moment of truth for all of us; facing one's selfishness, one's sins, one's inadequacies—and trying to look through the rationalizations which are used to cover up our failings (the "system," the "structure," etc.) to recognize how every betrayal of love weakens one and how increased weakness leads to new betrayal and so on in a vicious circle. It is a humiliating fact that for most of us this is the last thing we want to do. So I think it comes to something like this: one expresses his love in the manner and place and time which are open to him and which he opens to himself. He must bear the cross manfully in the limitation of vision, the failure of response, the imaginative blackout, whether these be around or *within* us. And finally we must have sufficient sense of gratitude to understand the source of these perplexing questions, these new insights. For these have not arisen in us spontaneously or been conferred on us by the world. In the last analysis these are the gifts of the Church! For all her real and present unworthiness she is our mother.

By now I probably have you sufficiently confused so I'll end before I do any more damage. What I started out to say was that I'm most grateful for your interest and sharing and for making me realize that the pat answers of a disembodied Christianity are completely meaningless. I'll remember you in my prayers; please include me in yours.

Love, in Christ our brother,

Joan

November 3, 1965
Dear Joan,

Thanks for your remarkable letter. There are so many things which can be said and which can't be said. I value your understanding and sympathy. Needless to say, I seem to be emerging (I hope!) from a serious crisis. It wasn't fun and still isn't. You are exact about the rationalizations of structure, at least in my case. Rather it's the "within" that irritates (not in the Teilhard sense of that word!). All the inadequacies, the self-seeking, the deceptions leading to selfishness—everything like this—and so disheartening because love is the guise.

Well, the one consolation is that you are able to share my thoughts and doubts and weaknesses. And I think I can share yours. The joy that comes from this sharing is the payoff which Our Lord speaks about in the hundredfold. How could it be otherwise? Since we can't live for ourselves alone, neither do we die for ourselves.

Here optimism dominates the situation. Perhaps that is the problem, that optimism, or humanism, or joy, forgets the real situation! For me, liberty and humanism are almost absolutes. And for you too, I think. Teilhard says "that just because I am a priest, I want to be the first to become conscious of all that the world loves, pursues, and suffers." Maybe in the throes of crisis will we come to say and live the same.

With much fondness,
Bob Eder

November 27, 1965
Dear Joan,

As I find myself kidding around with you too much face to face, I have decided to write and tell you how much I enjoyed Saturday's home fiesta. I write this same Saturday night, and though I know I will see you tomorrow in the city, I want you to know seriously of my appreciation.

Do you take after your father? Perhaps in your sense of humor, maybe in your civil rights attitude! He was great, especially with those folk and/or freedom songs. You were your true self—which I won't elaborate on now (but perhaps on another occasion).

The only regret I have is that it ended too early. I had been ready for an "all-day-all-night" fiesta. And then you had to leave early. Sometimes I can't believe it's all true. It seems unreal, but no matter what, I am grateful to you for it— I mean, of course, for your friendship and smile.

With love,
Bob

December 7, 1965
Dear Bob,

Since you released me from my promise to never write again I feel free in sending this to you. Anyway, I think writing is the more humane thing because at least you can sit down while reading. Someday we may even have the luxury of sitting down while talking. . . .

I made contact with someone (I'll explain later) and arranged for you to visit a school in New York. It's a Catholic school with a lay principal and they use the Montessori method in the first three grades. (The whole setup is very unusual so it might be worth visiting, in view of your new appointment.) And since I'm your secretary I'll go with you.

Also tomorrow night (Tuesday) watch Channel 13 at 8:30, *Who Speaks for New York.*

Love,
Joan

December 14, 1965
Dear Bob,

This is just to fill you in on what's been happening. I tried to call you but couldn't make contact. Thanks for your note. I always enjoy receiving them and sharing your ideas.

I'm disappointed about Friday evening but I understand your predicament. (I'll let you know how the evening goes.)

I went to Park Place on Saturday. Very dismal in the rain. One of the buildings is a real flop house (à la *Manchild*). The police were there, etc. I spoke to a young Negro girl who had been in and out of Kings County in twenty-four hours after having a baby! She told me never again— she was going to the clinic for pills, etc. I felt like a silent accomplice, but I just couldn't muster up a good reason for her not to practice birth control. One of the men decided to walk with me and kept taking my arm every time we crossed the street, and to make matters worse he kept calling me "doll" (not that I mind—but don't tell my father)! All in all it was an eventful day.

A friend of mine from a local community council has invited me to sit in on one of their meetings and share any ideas we have. But since you are the brains behind the outfit (there's no confusion of roles in my mind), I think you should come with me. How about it? . . .

I guess everything can be summed up in this quote from de Chardin: "Christ binds us and reveals us to one another. . . . What my lips fail to convey to my brother He will tell him better than I. What my heart desires for him with anxious, helpless ardor He will grant him—if it be good. What you cannot hear because of the feebleness of my voice—this I can confide to Christ who will one day tell it again, to your heart. . . ."

With love,
Joan

December 16, 1965
Dear Joan,

I don't know why I write to you today, as I probably will be seeing you Saturday. I guess it's because I want to, no other explanation needed! Your Christmas card was a beautiful surprise. I had thought that you were too disorganized to send cards so early, but I was disappointed, not unhappily. The surprise was matched and topped only by the choice of the quote from our dear mutual friend Père Teilhard. It is a thought which gives our life so much more meaning, so much more context, so much more richness. It reminds me of those other places in Teilhard where he with clear vision goes to the heart of things. Like where he speaks of all the communions of all of the people of the world, in the past, the present, and in the future, being just one Communion. And all the problems, sufferings, and heartaches of men being just one big heartache of Christ.

The thoughts you put in the letter reminded me of this, and reconfirmed me (Can I say it?) in my faith: that we don't live for ourselves, or die for ourselves. For that would be the most excruciating and meaningless existence of all. But that we are tied to one another somehow, and that we will know one another in Christ. And this is the meaning of our faith, and of our love. This is the main thought I wanted to share with you here in the letter. There are also some other things that you would want to know about (for all your curiosity!). For one thing, I wrote to X, thanking him for coming down to look the neighborhood over, and asking him to arrange a meeting for me with Y, the man he says has lots of savvy with the Board of Education. If X comes through with a get-together, I was thinking of bringing you to take down the more salient points. Anyway, you would lend an air of the jovial—so that we could talk in a relaxed atmosphere, etc. Also, I was thinking about your experience with that "friendly" man last Saturday on your favorite block. Although it probably will prove to be a chapter in your future book (better, "novel")—something akin to *Manchild,* but more earthly—I kind of feel (what English!?!) it's not so good for you to be alone on your rounds.

Know what I mean? If not, read or reread *Manchild*, page . . . ! Whatever happened to my stoical Cecilia? Really, I would not want anything to ever happen to you. It would look bad for the parish! No, you know, I really care about you, yourself. Please be careful. For Christmas I am trying to figure out what you would like, or what you could use. I have a number of things in mind, but I can't decide. It looks like I'll wind up presenting you with a number of things, none of which is extra-special, even though I should like it to be.

Hope this letter gets to you before Saturday, as I wish you would take to heart my suggestions about being careful on Park Place. And then, if you don't get it before Sunday, if I do happen to appear for the party, I will have to repeat everything above by word of mouth. So . . .

See you soon.

With much fondness,
Bob

December 20, 1965
Dear Bob,

Thanks for coming over on Sunday. I really appreciated it. So far, no repercussions from the "establishment," only undercurrents, and who cares for that! I agree wholeheartedly with your thoughts about community and have been doing a lot of thinking along those lines myself. So often we neglect the "vision" aspect of our work in our overconcern for effectiveness, etc. Without this central concept of vision it is impossible to have a vital sense of community. To me this is the most relevant thing: a group of people joined together around a common vision, sharing a great hope in common, and helping each other to see life as the Gospel exposes it to us.

It's a wonderful thing how we have grown in our capacity for relationship, not only with each other, but even with the most unlikely people. (Of course, as soon as we are open to relationships, we are also open to a greater degree of sufferings and problems.) But the good far outweighs this, and finding in each other's strength the courage to go on is also part of the hundredfold. How this sense of community has evolved in our lives I don't know. To me, it was a moment of grace, undeserved and unexplained! All I know is how thankful I am. As I see it we must bring this vital, real testimony of community to the people we live and work among, otherwise any group can do what we're trying to do. (It is precisely this other dimension which is our only reason for being or doing.) Working toward this sense of community and bringing to it all the energies of mind and heart that we can summon is the only assurance that we will be ready for long struggles, for many pressures, for fidelity, for death, and perhaps even for love.

Anyway, thanks again for coming over.

Love,
Joan

January 3, 1966
Dear Joan,

I am determined to write you a letter which I won't rip up. The last one I wrote ended up in the basket, because while it tried to say some important things, it did so badly and tritely. So don't feel bad, it was no loss. I do wish we had got going Tuesday after the Eucharist. Things dawn only after a while, and then when you are bursting to say them, it is too late. I found that our walk on the boardwalk toward the end of our day expressed so many things we didn't get around to in the conversation. It was a continuation of the Mass, because it said so much about community and unity of purpose and ideals. . . .

Maybe that's the reason you were so quiet afterward. Everything else seemed so trite and erratic and trivial. Even the music. We are all agreed that we ought to do it again, soon. . . . Sometimes the only thing you can say about a group like ours is that it is providential. Why should all of us, each from varied backgrounds, find ourselves thrown together and discover that each has so much in common? One of the group said something else very apropos on this, that it is the work of the Holy Spirit, bringing people together, all with common desires and aspirations. The point can well be seen with those first Jesuits, Loyola, Xavier, *et al.*, even though there is no comparison intended according to intelligence (for you maybe, but not for us!) or ability. Still the point is well taken. Suddenly five or six men find themselves in Italy at a certain time, facing grave problems. You might say the same for our group. For that reason, with St. Peter, I can say "it is food for me to be here." *A proposito*, I read *The Little Prince* a second time. I liked it better the first, because I guess I went nice and slow and got a lot more that way. It is a beautiful book. There is a section where the Prince is talking to a fox, with whom he becomes fast friends. The fox tells the Prince one important thing: that everything essential is invisible, *i.e.*, what is important to the heart can only be seen by the heart. And so the important thing about the flower that the Prince has on his faraway planet is that the Prince is responsible for it, that he has tended it, and loved it. "Men have forgotten this truth," said the fox, "but you must not forget it. You become responsible, forever, for what you have tamed. You are responsible for your rose. . . ."

What insight! Without kidding around, I think that answers a very profound philosophical question on how to reconcile one's individuality with the millions of other persons and things in the universe. The passage is tremendous. I have the book here for you. Maybe on Saturday when you come around you can bring me some of those books you have long been promising, and I'll make an exchange.

Really, I don't even care if you don't bring those books, I want you to read this one. 'Til then . . .

With love,
Bob

January 5, 1966
Dear Bob,

I wanted to write you sooner but somehow couldn't find the appropriate words (like the letter you tore up, everything seemed trite!). However, I do want you to know that the Mass on Tuesday was one of the most wonderful experiences in my life. Because of that Mass no other Mass will ever be the same. There's so much more I'd like to say about it but you can read between the lines. You never cease to amaze me. I was so surprised when you mentioned *The Little Prince*. L loves that book and is constantly writing me quotes, etc., from it. Her latest one: "It is because you have lost so much time on your rose that has made your rose so important and so you are always responsible for your rose . . ."

Coming back to the old theme: there are still so many questions which need answering. But it seems to me that to answer these questions is nothing less than the task of life itself. And so I am indeed fortunate in having you by my side to help me see life as the Gospel exposes it to us and then in giving me the courage and determination to be faithful to our vision of things. To quote Teilhard again: "Christ gathers up for the life of tomorrow our stifled ambitions, our inadequate understandings, our incomplete or clumsy but sincere endeavors. And if all this is so, we can indeed die with our ideal. We can be buried with the vision we wanted to share with others."

I especially like what you said on your Xmas card. It reminded me of something I read to the effect that because we do or try to do the best we can (though we may sometimes fail), a little more health is being spread in the human mass and in consequence a little more liberty to act, to think, and to love. And as you said, this is worth everything that might result.

There are in the lives of all those who take the chance on Christ's word and Christ's community certain obstacles and enmities and ignorances, hardnesses of heart, etc., such things as poor health or simple orders of obedience. But regardless of this there is for us the responsibility clearly seen to move forward, determined to know, determined as well to listen, to admit the wisdom of others.

And in the place appointed us, determined also to make a difference.

This letter is kind of fragmented but somehow I feel that you always understand what I am trying to say. So, for the New Year, peace, joy, hope, and love.

With love,
Joan

January 30, 1966
Dear Bob,

I want this note to reach you on Monday morning—your first day back on the job. How can I thank you for sharing your vacation with me and for all the wonderful moments we've had together? The truth is: I couldn't begin to thank you!

I'm listening to Joan B. as I write and delighting in a magnificent day. How I'd love to be out walking with you right now. Even though you are not here your presence is so strongly felt. I guess because I don't really ever leave you completely, Bob.

I feel so intimately a part of you that every action and word of yours is something sacred to me. Can you understand that? It is not a question of being intimate only during an isolated act, *i.e.*, lovemaking; because even that can

be something selfish. Rather, the minutes and hours we
have shared together, the thoughtfulness and tenderness we
have shown to each other, or simply the willingness to be
ourselves—for the sake of the other—assures us that we are
already intimate, and making love can only be the culmina-
tion of all this. As I see it, lovemaking is a total act embracing every minute of one's day. And I think Fromm was
right when he said people think they want intimacy; but
actually they avoid it all the time, because in order to confront another person with intimacy, you have to be willing
to show yourself and to be yourself, to shed that image you
like to protect. It requires a certain readiness to see oneself
as one is and to see another person. It requires even a certain sense of humanity to let a person be and to let oneself
be—without being indignant or over-tolerant.

Your sister was wonderful, Bob. She was willing to accept
me as I was and am and for that I am most grateful. She
made everything seem so normal and matter of fact. The
truth is that many times I can't see or think clearly simply
because of the pressures within and without the community. So you must continue to be patient with me and help
me.

Why don't you invite someone else to come on Thursday,
if you want. That way I can talk to you while the other person talks to Francine. I'm so selfish! Don't forget to be over
at St. Paul's early, if you can.

Con todo mi afecto,
Joan

February 6, 1966
Dearest Joan,
It is so painful for me to be apart from you. I thought of
you all day, ever since I left you on Saturday night, and I
want so much to be with you twenty-four hours each day,
seven days a week, for ever and ever. How could I ever de-

serve your love? It is pure grace, absolute favor. It makes me tremble to think of it. That is the reason why I become cold and start to shiver.

I want to tell you, and so often I can't, how dear you are to me. I want to use Shakespeare's sonnets, not only these but everything in the world that is true, good, and beautiful to repeat for me those words, "I love you." I want to fire them into your heart and I want to live my whole life repeating them to you. I thought I could tell them to you by phone tonight but by the time I was able to get back to the rectory, it was 9:15. I had thought it 8:15. When I rushed upstairs to the phone, I was completely dejected by the miscalculation. I went to a meeting then—about thirty priests—to discuss our neighborhood work. It was a good chance to work out some new approaches outside the structure, and almost everyone was happy with the results. We are going to have a team down there every day to press the housing issue, so as not to lose the momentum. Joan, you will be glad to know Sol Alinsky's name was by far the most prominent name dropped, and that the most frequently! By the way, didn't you promise me his two books? Ohhh! Keeping everything good for yourself!

I want so much to give my entire self to you. I want you to own me completely, to know every facet of my being, to know my joys, my secrets, my past, my present, my future, yes, even my sins, as long as I can receive your love and give you mine. I start to cry when I think of the intensity of our love. It is like Christ's love for us, and in fact it is through you that I can love Him like never before. For I am sure that neither life nor death, nor anything else can separate me from you and from your love. I feel so bad therefore at not knowing when I can see you and touch your hand and look into those dangerous eyes, and see your left eyebrow turn up, and by means of these, look into your very soul which I love so deeply and passionately. I feel bad that you are away from me even for one day, for one hour, for one second. That is the truth, Joan, my love and my very life.

And yet I want to love you more and more, with my love increasing like a geometrical progression, until I love you with the very heart of God, until I stand up and call your name, and you come running and we make love forever in God's sight. Can you understand this? Oh, I know you can, even better than I.

So then, my beloved above anyone, anything else, may this letter take my place with you, when I can no longer see you whether on Monday or Tuesday, and may it tell you things that I am prevented from saying by that horrible wall which surrounds you. You are soul of my soul, life of my life, bone of my bone, flesh of my flesh.

With my heart,
Bob

February 14, 1966
Dearest Joan,

How could I ever stop telling you I love you? I'd rather die first. How much your card meant to me! How much just seeing you means to me! How lucky I am, Joan. Why should someone like you come to me and explode my petty self-centered world to smithereens, and open my eyes to your love and goodness? Why should I be allowed to hold you in my arms and love you? Only God knows, but even in my ignorance I am eternally grateful. Please believe me.

I want to call you this afternoon and tell you what I feel and write now.

With all my being,
Bob

February 21, 1966
My dear one,

This is my prayer—that our love may grow richer and stronger day by day, that it might be rooted in all wisdom and knowledge and discernment, that it might be founded on Christ's love for us, of which it might be a sign to all, that it may support us and make us grow, that it might reach its climax before God Himself—this is my wish on your birthday, dear Joan!

> With deep love,
> Bob

February 21, 1966
To my beloved,
    Would you accept my poor love?

> Bob

February 21, 1966
Dearest Joan,
    May I share your smile and joy? Please share mine! I love you, Joan!

> Bob

February 27, 1966
My dear one,
    Loving you is the most important value for me.

> Bob

Sunday night, February 27
Dearest Joan,
    The hours pass so slowly without you. I am here thinking about you, hoping by this time (10 o'clock) you are now tightly tucked away in bed. What a joy it is for me just to gaze on your face when your eyes are closed! And how much I want to be with you, to hold your hand and to kiss you. Please help me not to be selfish. I just want to love you forever and my prayer is just *that*. I have just finished reading several pages from Philip's St. Matthew's Gospel. I read Our Lord's words and I want to read them with you

and to you, because I know our love is genuine in His sight. May I love you continually—forever? How can one separate (platonically) the "now" from the "hereafter"? Loving you now is proof I will love you hereafter. May God increase our love until death, and then, even then, add power, intensity, and more strength to it.

My dear one, let us love one another, because love comes from God and in this we know we are His children.

In our love,
Bob

March 6, 1966
Dear Bob,

So far, no overt action from the Establishment on the matter of phone calls. To compound the confusion I receive many "business" calls from the college or from presidents of different groups, etc. And this only points up the ridiculousness of the existing situation—"no phone calls during Lent"—as if life comes to a halt for everyone during Lent.

I'm not upset (in the sense of being nervous) about receiving calls or about what the superior will say to me. In fact, I much prefer a direct confrontation. However, what does upset me is that so many sisters, while not accepting or believing in these antiquated rules, have been so crushed by the total institution that they cannot bring themselves to openly reject them and make their true feelings known to the authorities. It also upsets me to see so many good people depersonalized or cast into the mold of passive-dependent personality types. The total picture seems so depressing. What is needed is certainly more than a structural modernization of traditional religious orders, and yet even this structural modernization seems out of the question for many years because so many superiors and bishops appear to be completely, totally, and hopelessly out of it. It's not that I'm basically disrespectful of authority (as you

know) but I am distrustful and disrespectful of those superiors who maintain a total institution or a fortress impregnable to the world!

Yesterday, one of the sisters asked me a few key questions
about the summer and what I wanted to do. I told her I
was seriously thinking of leaving the community (without
going into any other details because she wouldn't have the
ego strengths to understand!). She launched into a big
speech about my role in the community and how necessary
and important I am, etc., etc. (I don't believe it, however.)
When all was said and done she admitted to me that she
has spent years trying to convince herself that she should
stay but has never been able to resolve the matter completely in her own mind. I don't feel like going into it now
so let's talk about it another time.

Anyway, all of this is beside the point. The main point is
that I love you very much, Bob, and don't think I can live
my life without your physical presence. How unique and
wonderful it is that the two of us think together in practically everything that makes up spiritual activity and the
interior life—not to mention human activity. I wanted so
much to be able to talk to you on Saturday evening but it
would have been dangerous under the circumstances, and
seeing you for just a few minutes in the afternoon only
made matters worse. I'm looking forward to meeting you on
Wednesday and I'll try to get there before 3:30. (Meet me
inside the main door and hope that we don't meet anyone
we know! I don't care anyway.) As you said once before,
everything cedes to our love and I accept and believe that.

But you must help me not to be afraid. Sometimes I become terribly frightened and then when you put your arms
around me it disappears and I wonder what I was afraid of
in the first place.

Writing to you is such a poor substitute for talking to
you. I was thinking back on the nice day we had on Thursday and it really didn't matter who was there because you

were the only one I could see or think about. How can I thank you for sharing your love and your life with me?

With all my love,

Joan

March 7, 1966

Dear Joan,

What a beautiful, meaningful letter you sent today! I read it over and over because it showed me that for all the difficulties (restriction on telephone calls, etc.) the one thing that matters is our love. All else becomes of no importance.

Joan, I am thoroughly convinced of our love. To me, it is the most wonderful thing that has ever happened! I lay awake last night(around 1 a.m.) thinking of it, but above all, of you. The night we spent on Thursday said so much, the confidence we placed in one another, the simplicity, the beauty, the naturalness—all of these confirmed me in my position, and have dispelled the darkness created by fear, social pressure, or conformism.

You are so beautiful to me, your physical beauty, your mind, yes, your soul, even your arrogance(!), your optimism, your smile. Would you allow me to share your life? I do so much want to take you for my wife and make you happy. I want to live for you, and through you, for the whole world. Forgive me if I am being selfish, I really don't think I am.

I can't wait to see you on Wednesday. Would you smile at me, just once? I will be so happy! Just like you did when we had lunch à al Polynesienne!

Love,

Bob

March 21, 1966

Dear Joan,

After calling you from [a neighboring rectory] this afternoon, I stayed there for supper. I thought of you all through the afternoon, on my way home, and now I will go

on thinking of you, and loving you, Joan. How I regretted
not being able to tell you how I love you over the phone.

To tell you the truth, nothing interests me any more, except you. I do worry about you and I miss you so much.
Please be patient with me. If I do anything, I want you to
help me, and to be with me; and if I do love anyone, I want
it to be with you and through you. How selfish I know myself to be. In spite of your denial, it is true. And I know that
only through you do I have a chance of loving and of sacri-
ficing myself and escaping that self-centeredness which de-
stroys and takes all meaning out of existence.

You are my "yes" to the world and to God. You are the
only thing I am certain of, apart from God in Jesus. It reminds me of the answer Sister Jacqueline gave to her critic
who accused her of being a relativist. "The only thing I am
certain of," she said, "is that God loves me."

Please help me to love. I want very much to love people
and to help them. Forgive me for implicitly criticizing some
of the brethren, but work which is depersonalized, however
efficient and tiring, leaves me depressed. So too does any
theory of the apostolate which "compensates." Compensation need not take form in new cars or South Sea excursions.
It can, it seems to me, also appear in fraternities. God
knows we are all trying, and our human nature surely needs
aids and helps, but maybe things like the fraternity could
gain from being honest. It is the reason why I have dropped
out. Remember that beautiful evening we spent together
standing in the yard, when you said how important it was
that we admitted we didn't have all the answers. It is true.
Some things never will allow answers, but that is all right as
long as we are true to ourselves. You have made me true
and genuine to myself, but I need your help so much for
the future. Without it, without you, I will die. To die—
there are so many ways of doing it—some, many, are already
dead. God knows it is not their fault. That is why it is so

sad. Many in this neighborhood have been put to death by poverty and squalor and hopelessness. Many Catholics are dead, killed by hatred and coldness and structural meaninglessness. That is the great thing about our love—it is fertile and life-giving. No surprise, then, for my unabashed joy and naive optimism. "Therefore choose life!" All of these things become clearer every day. I feel so liberated and peaceful. I know you feel the same.

I am going to try to keep this letter a surprise for you. You should receive it on Wednesday morning, and when you read it, know that I will be thinking about you, and loving you.

Affectionately,
Bob

April 15, 1966
Tuesday
Dear Bob,

I want you to read M's letter. She says exactly what L said about *my* being responsible for your life and for the decision we make. It kind of scares me, Bob, to have this complete responsibility and to know that *my* decision will decide whether you leave the priesthood or not!

I guess I'm tired and the letter came at a bad time but I accept it as written because I know her sincerity: she is thinking only of us and not all the other incidentals like the community, etc.

I'm not wavering in my love for you, Bob. That is one of the absolutes in my life, but please help me to have the courage to stand by our decision.

With love,
Joan

May 4, 1966
Dear Joan,

It has been too long since I wrote you last. I have just finished Mass. I suppose many people would not want to think that our love is justified or legitimate. And coming from a conservative background myself, I can understand how they must feel. But the reality of our love is that it is integrated. When I love you, I love God and serve Him. When I am selfish in some way with you, I am selfish with Him. Love and sin stand out so sharply for me. When you attended the Mass last Saturday morning, I was so happy because it meant we were together in an act of love, for God and for one another. I hope you didn't feel ill at ease, because it was I, the priest, celebrating Mass.

Most people either deprecate or deify marriage. Catholics do the former, materialists the latter. Forgive me for being identified with the second group. I see it really as being a way of loving you, in complete accord with the Gospels and with Our Lord's injunction to love one another as He has loved us. I have trouble understanding a person who does not love someone as we love each other. Those who say they are going to love "all men" will likely love no one but themselves. Or, as Pascal says, those who want to become angels when they are really men, wind up as beasts.

For the first time in my life I have experienced love—I have experienced love—forgetting myself, social pressures, the army, and whatever.

We are like Abraham who God called to leave his family, his town, his people, to trust in God's love, and to go into a strange country and to a strange people, and live on trust alone, on love alone. We have risked all, and we have been given immeasurable return.

So, my love, I wanted to tell you these things, and to be with you on Thursday morning, when I cannot see you with my eyes, and when I miss you so much. I do long to see you Thursday evening, and to tell you face to face those things which I feel and know in my heart.

With all my love,
Bob

Monday night, May 16, 1966
Dear Joan,

Retreat has begun. Msgr. C promises to be good, with emphasis on group discussions. The matter we talked about on the phone has occupied my mind, and though it is unpleasant, I am glad for the chance to do some serious conscience-searching. It is unpleasant for me, honey, because I tend to apotheosize myself, completely without sin or other imperfection or stain. And that is not the reality. You show me who I really am, and I stand in amazement that you could still love me. I want to say I'm sorry, that I don't want to repeat such things again, but the words have so little meaning. I feel so low. You have shown that I cannot rely on my own words, that we must rely on His Word, and His strength. Joan, please accept my sorrow and please know how much I love you and want to make you happy—even though I succeed beyond expectation in doing the opposite.

With love,
Bob

May 17, 1966
Dear Bob,

Your letter arrived today and I was so happy to receive it. I, too, want to be with you every second and find the time apart from you so painful. To me our love is so liberating and so creative. Although at times I find myself caught in the bind of "limiting complexes," desires and anxieties, this is only a minor fact. The major fact is our love.

To be mature and honest in the present, as we have tried to be, seems proof enough that we will be able to live this way in the future. Not operating at the level of the external (which would be so easy) but trying to cut through to the inner dimension of reality.

I'm sorry that I upset you the other night on the phone. At first, I wasn't going to say anything to you but somehow I felt this would be interjecting a false note into our relation-ship. I thought of what Fromm said about people who think they want intimacy and actually avoid it all the time. Be-cause they are unwilling to show themselves and to be themselves they can never confront another with intimacy. It is precisely because we are so intimate that I feel I can share everything with you without having you become in-dignant or over-tolerant with me. And I love you all the more for your trying to understand me.

I was thinking of what you said on Saturday about our pushing the "new Church" to its limit. Since love is the virtue of a kingdom in process and since the Christian tradi-tion has always maintained the primacy of the spirit over law, I feel very strongly that our love and marriage in Christ has something important to say about the Church and to the world. Any sort of silence which might proceed from suspicion or expediency or embarrassment is a be-trayal—willed or inadvertent as the case may be—of the greatness of Christianity and our love. To be alert and open to the salvific implications of the moment and of our place in the "new Church" is not an easy task but one that seems demanded of us. Perhaps this explains the unusual depth and strength of our love.

My brother called me last night and, of course, isn't too happy about what we plan to do. However, we did have a good talk and he wants me to go out to supper with him. Carol is shocked to pieces (I should expect this reaction by now, but somehow I never got used to it) and I'm a little annoyed that they were told because I wanted to tell them myself. Pat seems to have transferred her dim view of the matter to Joe because he asked me to wait a year and to live at home, etc. I'm not happy about Carol's knowing so early because she has several friends who have relatives in the community and I have the horrible feeling that she will talk. I'm going home on the 28th and Joe said they would all be over. (Actually I'm dreading it and have mental images of the day: Carol looking at me in shocked amazement, Patrice crying, and my mother and father feeling bad, etc.) My big worry is that they will slip and say something in front of Patrice. I love you, Bob, and am praying and thinking of you during these days.

With love,
Joan

May 18, 1966
Dear Joan,

Can we meet on Friday? Maybe we can be together for a few hours before your four o'clock class. I'll call you sometime Friday morning and we can figure out some way?

Your letter was so clear, so beautiful. As you say, "any sort of silence which might proceed from suspicion or expediency or embarrassment" is not faithful to our love and its genuineness. With this thought in mind, I confided in Msgr. C this afternoon. He was disappointed, pretty much from the viewpoint of seminary rector. We talked for about an hour. He said he caught something of the validity and genuineness of the position, but that he could not understand it himself. He was great to acknowledge that my own conscience was the decider. He thought sign of openness and love was honest and right. It was a good discussion, as he did not hold back his frank criticisms, and I did not hesitate to tell him he was wrong. I am glad I told him. Now he knows we are acting according to our conscience, loving one another after the mind of Christ. Now I can understand how difficult it is for you to experience your family's sorrow and disappointment.

With love and affection,
Bob

May 25, 1966
Dear Bob,

I really wanted to send you an Anniversary card but didn't have one!

Actually if it weren't for your ordination and assignment here we would never have met. Somehow I don't think of your giving up the priesthood but rather of adding something to it. To me, your priesthood is intimately bound up with our love and I wouldn't want it any other way. De Chardin says we must follow our destiny and trust ourselves to it, even if we don't know where it is leading us. In his life he spoke of a deep-seated appetite calling him to all that is real. I like to think of that in our lives also.

> With love,
> Joan

June 2, 1966
Dear Joan,

I am beginning to like that "partial" security we discussed. We cannot be certain of such things as public approval, jobs, money, apartments. But it seems to me that we have made the right move in placing all our future in love and each other. I am happy to give up total security for our love, and though we lack material things and the confidence of some people, those things really do not matter. (Tomorrow I am supposed to call the personnel manager at the Office of Economic Opportunity.)

I did some more thinking, my darling, on the subject of the first night of our honeymoon. For me life is to be with you and love you. How irrational it would be without you, how meaningless, how unlivable. Sex has no meaning for me unless it is an expression of our love, and in the very act of making love, the value and beauty lie in the love and in the mutual giving and receiving. How happy we are in this realization! Even the anxieties and social pressures you mentioned in a recent love-filled letter give way to the inexpressible desire to give ourselves to each other in every way, physically, mentally, and spiritually. And so we are very happy. The life of God shows through one's smile and one's joy. I hope you see it in me. I see it in you, Joan, in your beauty and in your heart, and it is not two things, it is simply you. I want you to be so happy and to be loved. And after that nothing can disturb me or unsettle our life together. I miss you so much and hate to think that tomorrow I will be stuck here all day and unable to come to visit!

With much affection,
Bob

June 8, 1966
Dear Joan,

Late Wednesday night I sit here thinking of our love and our forthcoming marriage and its wonders.

I would like to describe it in detail, but I cannot. All I can do is repeat the words—I love you, Joan—and hope they will convey my deepest thoughts and sighs.

I want to spend my life in loving you and taking care of you. This is the reality which draws me infallibly toward LIFE, and this is what I choose completely, totally, with every power of my being.

With much love,
Bob

Pope Paul VI and Celibacy

Reverend Peter J. Riga

Father Peter Riga, thirty-four, was born in Buffalo, New York. He attended the University of Louvain (Belgium) from 1954 to 1958 and holds advanced degrees in philosophy and theology from that institution. Since his ordination in 1958, Father Riga has been a parish priest, hospital chaplain, seminary professor, theology professor at Notre Dame, and prolific writer. He is the author of twelve books and numerous articles for theological and other journals. In 1965 he received the "Man of the Year" award from the American Civil Liberties Union. During most of his priestly life he has been in the front rank of a variety of civil rights and peace movement activities. He is now on the faculty of St. Mary's College, Moraga (California), where in 1966 almost the entire student body rallied to his support with a strike threat, following an attempt by the Bishop of Oakland to have him removed because of his "liberal" views. He is perhaps best known for his commentaries on the papal social encyclicals.

At this time of crisis and change in the Church it is very difficult to assess the value of celibacy. The encyclical of Pope Paul VI issued on June 24, 1967, *Sacerdotalis Caelibatus,* makes this task all the more difficult. Already it is said that "Peter has spoken" and that further dissent is tantamount to disloyalty to the Church (American Catholic bishops). Such a method of procedure is bent much more on silencing the opposition than on convincing people of the essential value of celibacy. It is quite possible that it is still as valid as ever for the apostolate—for this is the *essential* consideration in the discussion concerning celibacy— but we shall never know if dissent in the Church is effectively crushed by the fiat of pontifical or episcopal authority.

Whether for good or for ill, this method of ruling the Church, at least in matters disciplinary, is anachronistic and counter-productive among both the lower clergy and the laity. On matters which affect them so intimately, they must be listened to with respect and open-mindedness. They simply will no longer accept the authoritative fiat of bishops in order to arrive at some form of consensus on what is beneficial or harmful to the apostolate. To the merit of Vatican II, *Constitution on the Church* stated clearly that the most fundamental constitution of the Church is the "people of God," structuralized indeed, but nevertheless part of the Church of Jesus Christ. If this viewpoint is taken seriously, then one must respectfully listen to the variant voices in the Church, freely deciding whether they are speaking with the Spirit or simply mouthing empty words.

There is a certain division in the Church. Increasingly, it is evident that the traditional practice and conceptualization of the Christian message as presented in the cultural and model forms of the early Christian period and that of the Middle Ages is completely unacceptable, not only to modern man, but to many modern Christians as well. If the divine word—which remains intentionally the same forever—cannot be translated *into and in* the experience of the modern world, it will remain a dead-letter for contemporary man, no matter how much authority is appealed to as the basis for accepting the divine truths. Divine they may be, but most men will never recognize them because they have not experienced the living Word. Modern man experiences the world in a way not known to Christians before him. The restructuring of the cosmos, technically, industrially, and socially, has shaped his present. The future only holds more radical transformations and experiences for man as he situates himself within the world. We must therefore speak differently about God in the context of our own experience of Him in today's world. The modern Christian has experienced a true "death of God" and is very disturbed because he does not know how to speak of God or how to address Him any longer. A simple "return to the sources" (by means of a certain traditional fundamentalism) can be—and for many has become—a naive form of escape from the world we live and experience.

Both the approach of Protestant biblical fundamentalists and Catholic papal absolutists must be rejected because these are simply escapes from contemporary problems. We need the Bible, we need the Pope, but we need both in an on-going dialogue with the lived experiences of the life of concrete man. We must re-read the Bible and tradition in the light of our own experience in which the whole Church (inclusive, evidently, of the whole structured episcopal body), under the influence of the Spirit, can move toward a definite consensus. It will be a time of tension as new methods are tried, others rejected, and still others revised, but it is a necessary tension if the Church is to emerge a healthy, growing organism. We must confront modern values and modern questions never before asked by men with the eternal Word of God. Our human experience is a necessary part of our incarnational reality in the world. It is part and parcel of our image of God (and we must have some image of God under pain of reducing God to nothing) which, of necessity, will and must change with a new age, a new culture, and a new way of confronting the world. God is the inexpressible, but must be expressed in the concepts man experiences in concrete life. Our religious experience is then conditioned by experiential social and cultural factors. Without them we would talk about and to God in a void. Therefore, if we refuse radically to transform the traditional conceptualization of God given to us from another and different age, then we condemn the faith to utter sterility and irrelevance. Life in the world literally nourishes our idea and conceptualization of God. The Scripture must be continuously and dynamically re-read in the light of our experience as a living community in the Church, and in the world. For we can have no direct relationship to God (at least normally) outside the mediate experience of the reality of our world and our brothers in the world.

Thus the great cleavage in the Church is between those who fear to engage this problem by its roots and those who know that the future of the Church is dependent upon such an *aggornamento*. The question of celibacy must certainly be ranked among these agonizing re-evaluations in the light of our experience today, not in light of what was valid for Christian ages of the past.

In the past two years discussions of priestly celibacy in the Roman Catholic Church have taken place. Not even the most radical theologian would have thought them possible three years ago. Sociological surveys in such Catholic journals as *Jubilee* and *The National Catholic Reporter* have revealed some of the personal feelings of priests on this, until now, "delicate issue." It has been "delicate" because most priests have simply been afraid to face the issue honestly, either because they have been brainwashed into actually thinking that it was *the* way to live the priesthood or because any public discussion would merit for them the label of "sexually disturbed," resulting in punishments or threats from the local chancery office. The surveys show what has long been admitted in private clerical circles, namely, a change in the centuries-old celibacy law is an imperative for the Roman Catholic Church in the twentieth century.

The following observations are not intended to "prove" that the relationship between priesthood and celibacy is neither scriptural nor of Divine law; we have long since by-passed that phase of the argument. We must examine celibacy *in its own right* to see whether, in the context of the modern Church, it can withstand the sole criterion of a relevant priesthood: the preaching of God's word in a modern world.

Vatican II marked a definite turning point in Catholic theology from which there simply can be no turning back regardless of rear-guard actions. Indeed, hesitance to accept this new evolution is in itself a major tragedy, since those who reject the implications of Pope John's council cannot and will not enter into the whole new future of Catholicism. The word "new" is used here in its strictest sense; there is little mileage to be gained from trying to show that such theology "was in the Church from the beginning," or that we are "simply going back to such and such an age," or that "this is what the Fathers taught," etc. We must face what we have refused to face for well over 500 years; we must accept and reconceptualize our whole concept of God and Christianity in the light of our proper experience of the twentieth century. The council marked the beginning, but only the beginning, of this momentous task. The whole future of our theology and Christian practice lies before us in all of its beauty and terrible responsibility. The central thesis is simply this: all human conscious experience is conceptual. But conceptual experience has a cultural form; that is, it arises exclusively within a social and historical situation. All human experience therefore has a cultural form: the specific form that human experience takes is determined by the social and historical situation in which it occurs. The faith, however, shares in the nature of all human experience. It follows that faith has a conceptual cultural form. In short, the concrete conceptual form that faith takes at any given time is determined by the social and historical situation in which it arises.

This point is paramount to Christians today trying to understand the faith and practice of the Church in the light of *their* experience and *their* age in *their* cultural milieu. It is to this supreme question that we must refer ourselves when speaking of celibacy.

II

What of the historical background of the celibacy question? It cannot be our objective here to investigate in detail the scriptural origins of celibacy for the simple reason that there is little in the Scriptures concerning this subject. In the Old Testament, all sexual activity rendered one impure so that the priests who approached the altar had to abstain—at least for a time—from sexual activity (Lev. 15:18; I Sam. 21:5). If the priest became impure, he had to wait till the morrow before he could resume his sacerdotal functions (Lev. 20:7). Virginity as a lifelong vocation—outside of the later Qumran community—was unheard of among the Jews. It was even considered as dishonorable since to have many children was the mark of God's favor (Gen. 30:23; Isaiah 4:1; 54:4).

The New Testament, however, does recognize the permanent state of virginity* of a man or woman dedicated to the kingdom of God. This is above all true of Jesus himself, the Blessed Virgin, and John the Baptist. It is presented to us as an eschatological witness, signifying that the things of time are passing; the virgin is a constant reminder that the kingdom is coming in which men will no longer marry (Luke 20:36). The man who accepts virginity voluntarily *for the kingdom* has a special grace which is not given to all (Matt. 19:12, 11-19, 29).

St. Paul's thought on virginity is complex. He praises the virgin who remains so in order to serve better the people of God, but he recognizes that virginity is a special gift which is not given to all. He accepts without any particular difficulty the fact that the presbyters, bishops, and other ministers of the Church are married. The dignity of the state of virginity accepted for the sake of the kingdom is exposed for us in chapter seven of the First Epistle to the Corinthians. It frees one for fuller and more complete service for the kingdom and brings to life the eschatological realities. He who is married is preoccupied with a wife and the things of earth. He who is a virgin is totally consecrated to the kingdom (I Cor. 7:26, 32-35). But this is a gift, a charism from the Spirit which is not given to all (I Cor. 7:6).

---

* We use the words "virginity" and "celibacy" as synonyms throughout this section.

Paul does not despise marriage. On the contrary, he up-
holds its dignity in a way undreamed of in pagan societies:
he makes it a sacred reality which imitates the love which
Christ has for the Church (Eph. 5:32; Col. 3:18; I Tim. 4:3;
5:14). As for the widows who cannot remain chaste, it is
better for them to remarry than to burn (I Cor. 7:9). The
important teaching of the Apostle in all of this is that we
follow Christ faithfully in any vocation in which Christ has
placed us (I Cor. 7:27-28). The important thing in Christian life is not that of charisms (necessary as these may be),
but life in Christ and fidelity to this life. Everything else,
inclusive of marriage, is secondary (I Cor. 7:29-31).

Paul considered it normal for the ministers of the Church
to be married; it never occurred to him to try to impose
celibacy on any of the Church's ministers. As a matter of
fact, a successful marriage was considered as one of the
criteria for the choosing of a bishop or other divine minister
(I Tim. 3:2-12; Titus 1:5-6).

Ministers of all ranks could freely choose marriage or
celibacy as they wished. In other words, during the first
four centuries there was complete liberty in the matter of
marriage—a universal "optional" celibacy. Thus, the words
of Clement of Alexandria (about A.D. 200): "The state of
marriage is a way of salvation for all, priests, deacons,
laity—if they use it correctly." * The Council of Gangres
(A.D. 345) condemned those who refused to assist at the
Mass of a married priest. The *Canons of the Apostles* (A.D.
400) excommunicated the bishop or priest who would abandon his wife "for reasons of piety."

In this regard there is an interesting story told by Socra-
tes, a Church historian.† He notes that at the beginning of
the fourth century there was already a move to demand
clerical celibacy. The Spanish bishop to the Council of

* *Stromata* I, 3, C.12 (P.L. VIII, Col 1189).
† *Hist. Eccles.* 1.1, C.11 (P.G. LXVII, Col 101).

Nicaea (A.D. 325) attempted to introduce the idea of obligatory celibacy by Church law. An Egyptian bishop—himself a celibate—St. Paphnuncius, protested this action since
he thought it would be imprudent and difficult to maintain.
Celibacy, he said, was a personal vocation and subject to a
free choice. This ecumenical council continued to permit
marriage to bishops, priests, and other ministers of the
Church.

Clearly, some of the greatest bishops and doctors of the
early Church were married. Gregory the Elder (A.D. 374)
was bishop of Nazianus when his son and successor, St.
Gregory Nazianus, was born (A.D. 330-386). Gregory of
Nyssa continued his married life after his consecration (A.D.
372).

It is also true, however, that there were a good number of
celibate ministers in the Church throughout this period, as
well as those who ceased marital activity after their ordination or consecration. Both Eusebius of Caesarea and St.
Jerome are witnesses to this tradition.* During the fourth
century the majority of the bishops of Thessalia, Greece,
Macedonia, Egypt, Italy, and Western Europe either were
celibate or discontinued a married life after consecration. A
letter of Synesius of Cyrene (A.D. 414) clearly attests to the
common respect and dignity for both the married and the
unmarried clergy. He himself would not accept episcopal
consecration if it meant separating himself from his wife. In
fact, he was permitted both marriage and the episcopacy.†

Church legislation, however, was instituted to regulate
the marriage of her ministers. The first rule was that they
had to be married before ordination or consecration. The
set rule was that marriage was permitted to the ministers of
the Church before the diaconate.‡

* Cfr. Jerome's *Adversus Vigilantium*, C.2 (P.L. XXIII, Col 341).
† See his letter, CV (P.G. LXVI, Col 1485).
‡ See the letter of Pope Siricus (391) *Epistola* 1 (P.L. XIII, Col 1137).

Another rule stipulated that the clergy had to be monogamous, that is, they were permitted to marry but once. If a minister became a widower, he could not remarry. He was not permitted to remarry under penalty of degradation from the clerical state. The early Church frowned upon second marriages as a scandalous giving in to the passions.

As is evident even today, the Eastern Church's legislation on marriage evolved differently from that of the Western Church. In A.D. 420 a law of the Emperors Honorius and Theodosius forbade the clergy from separating themselves from their wives under pretext of religious need. Justinian in the West was much more severe, not only forbidding marriage to bishops but also excluding fathers of families from the episcopal dignity. Those who were married but without children could become bishops only after separation from their wives. In the final analysis, a celibate was to be preferred for the episcopacy over a married man. Justinian's reasoning was clear: a bishop was to be totally dedicated to his people, not to any particular family of his own.* As in other early practice, priests were permitted marriage if they had been married before ordination.

The Eastern Council of Trullo (A.D. 692) was less severe in regard to bishops and in many respects simply endorsed what the Code of Justinian had proscribed. It criticized the Latin Church by condemning those who attempted to take away the right of priests and lower ministers to marry, as well as those who, under pretext of religion, left their wives after ordination. This council did make some concessions to the Latin Church by forbidding sexual relations to the priest about to engage in the divine cult as well as to those clerics traveling with their wives in Latin countries.† There has been no substantial change from that time to the present in the Eastern Church.

* Codex Justinanianus, 1.1, tit. III, lex 41, no. 1–4.
† *Mansi*, II, Co. 11.

The Western Church developed in an entirely different direction, due mostly to the intervention of the popes and Western councils who made (after the fourth century) clerical celibacy an obligation. The first evidence we have is a council held at Elvira in Spain (about A.D. 300), which demanded absolute continence from bishops, priests, deacons, and even minor ministers. As we have noted above, the Spanish bishop Ossius attempted to introduce this into the General Council of Nicaea in A.D. 325, but this was firmly rejected in favor of the traditional interpretation and discipline.

Western councils at first attempted to make celibacy voluntary but finally ended by making it obligatory.* It became obligatory during the second half of the fourth century under Popes Siricius, Innocent I, and St. Leo I in their letters and *Decretales*. Thus various councils held at Carthage in Africa in A.D. 390, A.D. 401, and A.D. 417 formally enforced this, with that of A.D. 401 forbidding married priests and deacons their marriage. The same laws were made by the Council of Orange in France (A.D. 441) and that of Turin in Italy (A.D. 398).

The argument for obligatory celibacy was complex, but the essential reasons were few: as an example to widows, scriptural arguments (principally Rom. 8:9; I Cor. 7:29), and the incompatibility of the ministry with conjugal activity.†

In practice, the ministers had to swear a *conversio* declaring their intent to be celibate before ordination to sacred orders. This put them in the same category as public penitents, that is, those for whom the exercise of marriage was forbidden (*v.g.*, Canon 22 of the Council of Orange in A.D. 441). Usually a time lapse was required between the *con-*

---

* See a Council at Rome in A.D. 386, Canon 9: "we desire that priests and deacons not live with their wives. . . ."
† Cf. P.L. XIII, Col 1181–1196.

versio and ordination as a sort of time of trial. Pope Gregory I speaks of this *conversio* as a general rule for all sacred ministers inclusive of sub-deacons.* The same was done at the Fourth Council of Toledo in Spain in A.D. 633.†

If these men were married, they had to leave their wives before ordination. These women received a special blessing and were then called *presbyterissae* or *diaconissae* and wore a special garb. They could not remarry even if their husbands died. For a time, however, these priests were permitted to co-habit with their wives in the same house (usually because of economic reasons), but because of evident abuse this was soon done away with.

With the Middle Ages there was a practical relaxation of these rules. Marriage was illicit but not invalid for all of the clergy throughout this period—with the result that most priests were in fact married. The councils held during this period constantly complained of these abuses and strove to correct them. Thus, various councils again strengthened the law of celibacy for the clergy (Soissons, A.D. 909; Augsburg, A.D. 952; and Poitiers, A.D. 1078). Such popes as Benedict VIII protested in the same vein (A.D. 1018) and reinforced celibate legislation. Priests and deacons were forbidden to marry or to live with a woman. Any children they might have were to be serfs of the Church and would be forever deprived of liberty, property, or inheritance (in order to avoid nepotism).

Yet there were always a few who persisted in the practice of the early Church in the name of personal liberty and freedom.‡ These efforts were effectively condemned and silenced. Nicholas II (A.D. 1059) deprived married priests of the right to conduct liturgical services. Leo IX (A.D.

---

* *Epistola* 44 (P.L. LXXVII, Co. 506).
† *Mansi*, X, Cl. 627.
‡ For instance, a small book by an unknown author, *Rescriptum seu Epistola de Continentia Clericorum.*

1049) made slaves of the women taken as wives by priests. Gregory VII made no new laws but vigorously enforced the existing ones, especially through his bishops and papal legates. Finally, the First (A.D. 1123) and the Second (A.D. 1139) Councils of the Lateran declared these unions to be not only illicit but also invalid. Here occurred for the first time the canonical impediment to marriage by the clergy (priests, deacons, and sub-deacons).

Once again, during the fourteenth and fifteenth centuries, there was more abuse due to various causes such as the black death, religious wars, the schism of the papacy. Luther made a clean break in this respect, along with the reformers of the sixteenth century. Since the Sacrament of Holy Orders was finally denied by the reformers, the celibacy of priests and ministers went by the board. Calvin, for instance, conceded that celibacy might be a useful vocation for service to the Church, but he saw it as existing on the same par with marriage.*

The Council of Trent reacted with vigor to this challenge, but for all practical purposes it simply reinforced the discipline already on the canonical books of the Western Church. Some of the council Fathers attempted to have the council define the incompatibility between marriage and ministerial priesthood in order to show that celibacy for the clergy was a divine obligation. Happily, the council simply repeated what was traditional in the Church: the Church has the power to demand celibacy of her clergy and to dispense from it when necessary, because celibacy is based on ecclesiastical law not on a divine imperative.† In this case, the traditions of both East and West were safeguarded. The legislation presently in vogue is substantially the same as that of Trent and the Second Council of the Lateran, preserved in Canons 16, 132, 987, 1072, 1114, and 2388 of the Code of Canon Law of 1917.

* *Commentaries on the New Testament,* on Matt. 19 and I Tim. 4:3.
† D.B. 1809.

III

We are perhaps now in a better position to examine the words of the Pope's encyclical, *Sacerdotalis Caelibatus*, issued on June 24, 1967. First it must be said that Pope Paul attempted to relate this ancient Western custom to the present. He was only partially successful since, in the final analysis, he proposed something which all in the Church accept and have always accepted—consecrated virginity for the kingdom—but managed to enforce it on the clergy of the West not on its own merits but by his apostolic authority. Most of the reasons he gave for celibacy are valid and beautiful but irrelevant to the issue of obligatory celibacy for priests. The Pope went further in this respect than any of his predecessors or any Church legislation: in the vocation of the priesthood, the person so called has *also* the charism of celibacy.

> The priesthood is a ministry instituted by Christ for the service of His Mystical Body which is the Church. To her belongs the authority to admit to that priesthood those whom she judges qualified: that is, those to whom God has given, along with other signs of an ecclesiastical vocation, the gift of consecrated celibacy. (par. 62)

If this is true, then the Eastern Church has a sort of second-rate priesthood. The Pope, however, gives this tradition some recognition in the encyclical (par. 40). Nevertheless, he cannot embrace both views since the matter of celibacy is not a question of variation of cultures or experiences —but a fundamental theological interpretation of the mystery of the person and the charism of the Spirit. Therefore, once he theologically defines the relationship between priesthood and celibacy, he is on the horns of a dilemma. As we have seen historically, the Pope's view comes very close to that opinion, rejected by the Council of Trent, which sought intrinsically to relate these two different vocations as something absolutely new in the history of the Church. The argumentation of the present Pope and those fathers of the council is strikingly similar. Their first argument (*v.g.*, John of Labura, Claude de Saintes, Michel de Medina, John Peletier) was that celibacy is a condition of this complete service of God and of the apostolate. A second argument was added: that the priesthood demanded a holiness of the greatest possible degree. Since the Old Testament required its priests to abstain from sexual relations at least during the exercising of the sacred functions in the name of "purity," how much more so for the priests of the New Covenant who are consecrated to the divine service for all days? Thus, the incompatibility between marriage and the priesthood. Marriage is not bad in itself (*cf.* par. 31 of the encyclical) but renders a man inept for the service of God. Consequently (and the Pope is very close to this position), celibacy is for the priest a duty based on divine law.

Perhaps one of the major criticisms is that, in an age when it is more and more agreed that authority within the Church must be exercised in a true dialogue with all the people of God, very little dialogue with those most interested (priests) went into the composition of the text. The Pope states that he consulted with other bishops (par. 2) but not with priests nor, *a fortiori,* the laity. Any sociological investigation made in this field almost has had to be done outside the Church structure proper, since all such investigations are held suspect. Yet there can be no proper understanding of the problem of celibacy without such an investigation, and it is astounding how little of such study went into the composition of the Pope's letter. Of the studies that have been conducted, particularly in the United States, a clear trend toward optional celibacy for the clergy is evident. Over 50 percent of all the clergy surveyed in the United States would like to see an optional celibacy, and what is perhaps more telling for the future, over 80 percent of the younger clergy surveyed wanted such an option. One cannot conclude much from such an investigation except to say that unless something is done in this regard, we will attract fewer and fewer vocations (already in heavy decline for a multiplicity of reasons) and continue to lose some of our most idealistic young priests. It is true, as the Pope notes (par. 49), that abolishing clerical celibacy will not numerically increase the number of vocations. Yet, this is not the right question to ask. What we ought to ask is whether under the present discipline of celibacy we can attract the best young men for the apostolate. Without judging what would be the "best" in the theoretical order (an impossibility, really), we must ask, given the present reality of modern life, *whether we like it or not,* can we attract the best young men for the priesthood by imposing celibacy? This is the heart of the problem, not the numerical increase in vocations. The argument of the Pope is rather circular:

> The cause of the decrease in vocations to the priesthood is to be found elsewhere, especially, for example, in the fact that individuals and families have lost their sense of God and of all that is holy, their esteem for the Church as the institution of salvation through faith and sacraments . . . (par. 49).

Surely this is a generalization which each generation repeats in its own fashion. As we pointed out in the beginning of this chapter, the heart of the whole problem is the inability of the Church to rethink her teachings in the light of modern experience. That is why the Pope has really failed to have a true dialogue with the Church and the world on the question of celibacy. Literally speaking, these people and the Pope are not speaking or understanding the same language. It may very well be that celibacy provides the best condition under which the priest can exercise his apostolate, but we shall never know as long as there is obstinate refusal to even re-examine this issue in terms of his experience.

In a true sense, the malaise here is more profound than the question of celibacy. At least empirically speaking, the quality of Christian life is no better or worse than that of that part of Christianity (East and West) which permits a married ministry. One simply cannot argue empirically from the quality of Christian life in Latin Christianity to show that it has produced the fruits of outstanding Christian existence. This alone would give grave cause for doubt to the Pope's insistence that celibacy is more appropriate for the life of the Church (pars. 26-34, "The Ecclesiological Significance of Celibacy").

The encyclical does not recognize what the modern secular world has long seen: the inalienable right of every human being to marry; this, as recognized by the popes themselves, is a divine right which no ecclesiastical law can completely take away from any man:

> Human beings have the right to choose freely the state of life which they prefer, and therefore the right to establish a family, with equal rights and duties for man and woman . . . (*Pacem in Terris,* par. 15).

And as Paul VI himself has said:

> Where the inalienable right to marriage and procreation is lacking, human dignity has ceased to exist. (*Progressio Populorum,* par. 37.)

If there is but one exception—albeit in the service of the apostolate—that right cannot be "inalienable." The Church can strongly recommend and encourage but can never force a charism which must be *continuously* and dynamically the free gift of self to the apostolate and the kingdom. How can the Church have the moral power to abrogate an "inalienable" right? The only legitimate theological response is that since she has the charism of the Spirit to make known to her children the will of God in this area, she alone can determine this for any period and culture. This indeed is a legitimate and convincing argument against which anyone who has any sense of the *Catholica* cannot argue. Yet we are back to the question which we posed earlier, namely, that it must be the whole Church which sees this value and arrives at a moral consensus on a general direction of the Church for a particular age. It seems rather evident from this argument that since the present legislation on celibacy will stand, those priests who wish to marry have the perfect right to do so at all times, and the Church clearly ought to recognize this right by dispensing them, with a minimum of inconvenience, to a worthy state as laymen within the Church. At least this much seems to be very clear from the discussions on celibacy over the past five years. It follows that a priest or religious who would marry, with or without dispensation, would commit no sin. Nor could the law effectively take away this inalienable right by any form of subterfuge, such as requiring a special form and not giving it when asked. Any Christian who would condemn a person for using this right is surely condemning God for having given that right, not to say sinning against Christian love. For the Church to keep this obligation as an option for her clerics is one thing; for her to obstruct or prevent those who wish to leave it *honorably* in order to marry is to commit a grave social injustice.

Not all that the Pope has written in his encyclical is worthless for the priest today. On the contrary, many of his points are quite valid from every point of view—even beautiful. The parallel existence of the priest with and in Christ (pars. 17-25) is at once theologically profound and will give food for serious thought to all those who wish to abolish completely this most precious charism in the present

Church. In this the Pope is quite correct in calling consecrated virginity for the kingdom "a brilliant jewel, and retains its value undiminished even in our time when mentality and structures have undergone such profound change" (par. 1). Indeed, this charism of the Spirit is more precious today than in the past, given the materialistic and atheistic trends of humanism in our day. The priest is needed as the "fullness of Love" (par. 24) in an ecclesiastical community which does not know love or how to love outside egotistical, familial, sexual structures. He lives now what all the Church will attain to in God's time and in God's way. He must love all of God's people, make each one of them *feel* and *know* that God loves him, has compassion on him, as symbolized in the gift of this man to the whole people of God. In a world which knows egotism, greed, and nationalism, the priest stands as one who has all men as his brothers, his love uninhibited by flesh, national origin, race, or color. His celibacy should intensify this feeling of eschatological witness (pars. 33-34) among not only the people of God but all men of good will. Christianity looks essentially to the future, is projected to God's future intervention in history (the Lord's *Parousia*), and as such the Church lives that tension of the "now" and the "not yet"; and yet, this "not yet" must surely come in the time and way which God has appointed. Thus the celibate is the charismatic leader who is the witness to this future hope, to this future of God and of man and who, like the Church, is the "sacrament of universal salvation." Such a value will not, cannot ever be, subtracted from the terrestrial life of the Church, and the whole Church in faith daily prays for such gifts of the Spirit.

There can be no dispute with the Pope by anyone who has any of this sense of the *Catholica*. He who would deny the existence and desirability of this value within the Church does have the full sense of the *Catholica*. Theologi-

cally, nothing could be clearer. What is not at all clear
—and the Pope's arguments do not convince—is that priesthood and this charismatic gift must be inseparable, at least
in the Western Latin Church. He recognizes this implicitly
by praising the Eastern tradition of a married lower clergy
(whose history we have seen above) in par. 40. In the next
paragraph (41) he rejects this separation in the Western
Church with the following argument:

> In any case, the Church of the West cannot weaken her
> faithful observance of her own tradition. And it is unthink-
> able that for centuries she has followed a path which, in-
> stead of favoring the spiritual richness of individual souls
> and of the People of God, has in some way compromised
> it, or that she has with arbitrary juridical prescriptions
> stifled the free expansion of the most profound realities
> of nature and of grace.

This is an impossible argument. We cannot judge what
was good or bad because we do not live in the past. What
alone we can judge, as a community, is our own experience
in the world and, in this context, whether celibacy and
priesthood must be inextricably united in the Western
Church. When the Pope argues for the present retention of
this rule by simply stating that it is unthinkable that what
was good for them would not be good for the Church of
today, he simply disregards the present life of the Church,
and therefore the real question: whether celibacy for priests
today will be profitably for the spiritual good of Christians
today. The Pope uses the same argumentation as did the
minority opinion of the commission on birth control. The
conservative view ends its investigation by stating: "For the
Church to have erred so gravely in its heavy responsibility
of leading souls would be tantamount to seriously suggesting that the assistance of the Holy Spirit was lacking to
Her."

The two arguments of the Pope and the minority view of

the commission on birth control are strikingly similar in
that they both argue by a literal fidelity to the past. We are
here at the root of the same difficulty which we have exposed at the beginning of this chapter. This inability faithfully to translate the intentionality of the divine Word
(under guidance of the Holy Spirit charismatically given to
the whole Church, inclusive of her structured hierarchy)
into the experience of the Church in a new sociological and
cultural world is at the very root of the whole problem.

The Pope denies that the ordaining of married men as
deacons represents the first erosion of the law of celibacy
for priests (par. 43). Yet, as we have seen, this is a unique
step in the clerical discipline of the West. From the fourth
century to the present, ordination was forbidden to a married man; or if he was married, he had to permanently separate himself from his wife. Nowhere has the Church of the
West ordained to the deaconate a married Christian man.
This new practice of the Western Church is an absolute
departure from tradition and no amount of denials can
gainsay this reality. If the Church has seen fit to set aside
—with little fanfare and disturbance—a tradition which is
over 1,700 years old, one wonders why it should be so
"shocking" to the people of God or to the supreme authority to suggest that, possibly, the time has come to lay
aside this obligation for priests as well? One simply does
not see the logic here within the context of the life of the
Church. Nor does one see why such a separation of celibacy
from priesthood "tears down that vigor and love in which
celibacy finds security and happiness" (par. 43). The security and happiness of the true charismatic celibate—layman
or priest—comes from the Holy Spirit to which the individual Christian responds out of love and sincere desire, not
from ecclesiastical coercion. One simply does not understand the attitude of those who are "shocked" or "grieved"
because of a desire to be a priest and to be married at the

same time. One thing is certain here: if we are to be serious in our ecumenical endeavors in the West, this problem must be confronted sooner or later since the Protestant tradition and experience has little or no place for a celibate ministry. We have here a whole Christian witness in the West which has survived and has been fruitful without the experience of compulsory celibacy. Any ecumenical endeavor is doomed to failure unless we are willing to accept this tradition within the communion of the *Catholica* of the Western Church. Since we are not seeking to "convert" them to Catholicism but rather to draw closer as communities with diverse experiences, we shall have to learn sooner or later that ministry in the West cannot be inextricably united to celibacy. This ecumenical problem is one which we cannot deal with here in detail but one which already disturbs many of our non-Catholic Christian brothers in the West.

The argument of the Pope that celibacy "evidently gives to the priest, even in the practical field, the maximum efficiency and best disposition, psychologically and affectively, for the continuous exercise of a perfect charity" (par. 32) is simply not to be proven empirically. Besides belittling the witness of married Eastern priests and the Protestant ministry, this argument cannot be proven on its own merit. We have today too many examples of doctors, astronauts, and even businessmen who are quite dedicated to their work while raising a family. This hoary argument is more and more of doubtful validity in our day and age, and not many will be convinced by it. The argument for celibacy is valid but must not be cluttered with worthless buttressing arguments which men of today see as doubtful. Celibacy freely accepted for the kingdom is an eschatological sign of the Christian future and a presence of universal charity in *this* man *par excellence*. All these arguments do not show, however, the necessity of mandatory conjunction of celibacy with priesthood. It is true that the Church's orientation to the world is not necessarily answered or understood by "logic" or "reason" (for she has the charismatic presence of the Spirit within her at all times), but at least we ought to leave aside all those past arguments for celibate priesthood which today appear as rather tenuous. The Pope does not often do this. In truth, the reasons he advances for the Church's honoring consecrated virginity for the kingdom are accurate, even poignantly beautiful. The only basic criticism, therefore, is of the fear of making this "beautiful jewel" optional for all of the clergy. One simply objects to the Church's making this charism of Christian existence, so necessary for the ecclesiastic community, obligatory for any class *qua* class within that same community. In this there is only tragedy for the modern Church in that she is both losing and failing to attract the best men for the service of God's holy people. It is a question to be investigated by the whole Church and a *consensus* must be reached. This consensus cannot be attained if, in an encyclical on the subject, all are called upon now to keep silent because "Peter has spoken." In view of the Pope's encyclical, any change in the present legislation is unlikely, but to impute disloyalty to those who may dissent will serve to create even more dissent.

This encyclical on priestly celibacy restates in selective apologetical arguments the "fundamental norm of the government of the Catholic Church." The disciplinary nature of its content removes it to the fringe of the infallibility charism, which requires from responsible Catholics the "internal assent" due to authentic pronouncements in Church matters. Such internal assent pertains primarily to the policy decided upon by the Church legislator and cannot extend to the dialogical process employed in the course of arriving at the final choice, unless one is willing to do violence to intellectual honesty. Thus, while accepting the choice as a matter of discipline, a Catholic is free to question the validity of the reasons adduced in favor of the choice, particularly when this is made not on compelling evidence of revelation or tradition, but on the basis of organizational imperatives.

Of all caducous documents which have come out from Rome in the last decades, this encyclical promises to be the ultimate embodiment; only *Veterum Sapientia* may compare with it in obsolescence potential, closely followed by *Spiritus Paraclitus*, another masterpiece conspicuously left in abeyance soon after its appearance. These and scores of similar documents, systematically and mysteriously ignored, have performed the paradoxical function of phasing out the very positions they portended to enhance. The question is: when will Rome agree to take the world (and the people of God) seriously. Let us repeat that the Pope, as ruler of the Church, has a legitimate claim to insist upon continued adherence in the Church to the celibacy rule and to demand it as a necessary condition for priestly ordination. However, the objection advanced in liberal circles prior to the promulgation of this encyclical appears to be all the more justified: the attempt to preempt all discussion on this most sensitive spot of a shaky structure is bound to generate a reaction far transcending this single issue. One doubts whether Rome is aware of the unexpressed but growing reassessment of the whole institution of the priesthood by Catholics all over the world. A recent study of laymen in Europe, North America, and Latin America, conducted at the University of California, Berkeley, cogently reveals that the thinking and advanced laymen in these areas identify in the priests and in the hierarchy the responsible agents of the present maladjustment and confusion in the Church today. Matured through the toughening crucible of competition and achievement in a technological milieu, a large number of intelligent and educated laymen feel clearly ahead of the priests and the hierarchy in the understanding of social and moral problems and openly question the "Church's" competence to exercise effective leadership, apart from the area of cult and good order. Were Rome more familiar with empirical research, it would have known that many educated Catholics have already resolved the problem of birth control. Any forthcoming pronouncement from Rome, whatever its content, will make no difference to them. The failure to perceive this totally new trend in the Church spells out the most tragic miss of an emergent process of norms and value formation within the Catholic community. The process of setting norms has changed and the function of legitimizing moral norms has progressively shifted from institutional authority to an enlightened communitarian consensus.

The encyclical elaborates on the "manifold suitability" of clerical celibacy in the conventional Church structure. An honest analysis of the problem cannot leave out the host of pragmatic considerations and concomitant problems which a change in the priestly celibacy rule would usher in: the problem of a just and dignified salary, the problem of redistribution of clerical control at the local level, the problem of a merit basis for clerical mobility, promotion, and retirement. In lieu of raising the multifarious implications of these issues, the familiar mechanism of displaced sublimation (celibacy is a "jewel") of a crisis situation obscures the problem at hand. Our times call for a more sincere, honest, and Christian view, which eschews political double talk and dialectical sophisms.

Three questionable assumptions pervade this encyclical.

1. An underlying reductionism of the family and marital experience to sexual activity and a subtle downgrading of marriage, the prototype and primordial sacrament which God himself conceived for man, versus the man-made mandate of celibacy for the Western priest of the fourth century, A.D.

2. The deviants from the Church's requirement are pejoratively commiserated as "unfortunate" victims unfaithful to binding obligations. Behind this paternalistic view, skillfully designed to underplay the evidence of massive transgression, lies a fallacy. For, when the encyclical appeals to the "magnificent wonderful reality" of those who apparently live their life of consecrated celibacy, including the saints, a minimum sense of honesty would call for the counterbalancing evidence of countless members of the clergy who systematically resolved their difficulties in this area ranging from open concubinage to legal marriage, mistresses, paramours, and platonic dating. And shall we not include the diluted forms of homosexuality and other forms of unwholesome sexual expressions in seminaries and religious houses, for which too much depressing evidence is at hand? The non-publicity of these widespread phenomena and the loyalty of the understanding flock which glosses over individual instances and subtracts them from notoriety is no excuse for knowingly stacking the cards and ignoring contrary evidence. Left out are the thousands of cases of more coherent and upright priests who have applied for dispensation of their celibacy obligation or who have left the ministry outrightly.

3. Blame is placed on the method of selection and induction into the priesthood. This is, in our view, the strongest corroboration of the fundamental point here: in an institution which is losing its meaning and function, no amount of screening and weeding will prevent the exodus from seminaries and the defection from the ministry. Very probably, this exodus will increase as the new generation comes of age, reared in a view of sex and human relations quite different from Rome's perspective—a generation which has seriously weighed afresh the morality of each human and social act, from premarital intercourse to fashion in dress, from the morality of a war of "containment" to the permis-

siveness of free speech and inquiry on university campuses. The seminarian who emerges from this generation has, in the inner autonomy of his conscience, unknowingly attained an identity which bears no resemblance to the virginity image of the priest of the past.

The celibacy problem, therefore, is but one symptom of the central moral problem of the Catholic Church as the institution-sacrament. Is this institution for man or is man for this institution? The encyclical equivalently states that, because of the traditional Western mentality and peculiar historical circumstances of the Roman Catholic Church, celibacy which, in the words of Vatican II, "is not indeed demanded by the very nature of the priesthood as evidenced by the primitive church and from the tradition of the Eastern churches," will be a functional requirement of Western Roman Catholicism, no matter what its cost to the human person hemmed in by the false dilemma of being a priest-celibate, or no priest at all. All great civilizations have imposed various controls on the expression of sexual energies in the interest of achievement, goal attainment, and control maintenance for the concerned societies. While the Church is quick to avail itself of viable formulas of history, it has never acquired the ability to persevere in its study of them and the agility to steer a timely course when the signs of time point to a new direction. It is a sad realization that all change in the Church has occurred under conditions of compulsion and inescapable survival pressure.

In the course of the sociological research study already mentioned, the mature laymen of Europe, North America, and Latin America, with surprising consistency, came out in favor of a married clergy as an optional form of ministry, and, even more surprising, this consensus included a sizeable percentage of "devotional" and conventional rank-and-file Catholics. If this evidence of a new degree of tolerance among the Catholic flock is matched with the evidence of the various exploratory inquiries conducted among priests in various countries concerning the celibacy of priests, grave questions emerged: what is the ecclesiastical value of this emerging *sensus ecclesiae* which, in a very controversial and interest-loaded question, bears strong analogies to the *sensus ecclesiae* which, upon solicitation from Rome, grounded the declaration of the dogma of the Assumption? What criterion will be used to discriminate between the acceptability of this sponsored "consensus" and the rejection of the emergent "consensus"? And should Rome, in a not too distant future, revise its position on this issue (as it most certainly will), what implications will the present categorical stand have on papal competence in moral issues (as well as on the prophetical function of the hierarchy)?

If priestly celibacy is indeed the brilliant jewel of the Church, there appears no reason why this jewel should be kept under lock and key and never exposed to the challenging light of the sun. If the testimony of many ministers in the Church is an authentic personal decision and not a passive submission to an arbitrary juridical prescription, why is the Church afraid to let the merit of this system manifest itself by giving equal option to our priests for a confirmed celibacy or a married priesthood? One would presume to predict that, given such option, the number of priests who would elect not to marry would be far greater than the number of those who would marry. The tremendous impact that this genuinely free choice would have on the Church is utterly beyond the imaginative possibilities of an administrative mind.

IV

The experience of most of the priests with whom I have come in contact is that they took on the burden of celibacy because there was no way of escaping it; in other words, the charism of celibacy for the kingdom has been imposed by Canon Law and what is the free gift of the Spirit is now encompassed within the confines of Church law.

It has also been shown that the experience of the present structure of the Catholic priesthood is both stifling and infantile. To be honest, this is slowly changing in many sections of this country, but not to a degree which will respond to the basic need of making the priest feel like a man once again. It is also to be feared that the present system of organization has so injured many of the older priests that it may be impossible to salvage them and that the younger clergy, sensing their unwillingness or inability for radical change of the present structures, are leaving in increasing numbers. It is one of the great tragedies of the modern Church that she is not losing her worst but her very best sons who, precisely because of their idealism, cannot square their experience as men of the modern world with the priestly structures in which they are obliged to carry on their apostolate.

These structures include, for the most part, the infantile functions of parish life, such as financial administration, a school system which is a drag on the apostolic formation of the *whole* parish, devotions and practices which are not only for a minute few but "for the saved." The parish is not a community with real ecumenical endeavors attempting to reach all persons within the confines of parish and diocese. The younger clergy see all this as a living death; challenge and idealism can be crushed by the "prudence" of the local Chancery office. What challenge do we offer the idealism of youth? Any deviation from even the slightest rigid standards of Canon Law are dealt with in a manner reminiscent of the medieval inquisition. When priests in Philadelphia can be expelled from the diocese or are sent to "homes of correction" for celebrating a meaningful liturgy in English, then one must actually laugh at vocation directors who complain that the present decrease in vocations is due to the selfishness of the present generation. Freedom is a *word* which is used for the relationship of the institutional Church with the world, but it is a word which is never taken seriously within the Church. Freedom of initiative for the clergy is something read about in the Conciliar documents of Vatican II, but if taken seriously will merit the priest a quick transfer or a formal rebuke "on the carpet."

The situation in the schools is not much better in this regard. Priests know perfectly well that they teach in high schools because, frankly, they are paid nothing. This whole army of professional civil servants (nuns, priests), is, of course, the reason why the mammoth school structure of the Catholic Church in the United States can function at all; the institutional Church justifies its actions since "it is doing the work of God."

Some of this might be acceptable to presently dissatisfied priests if, in reality, the results were commensurate with the talent and resources expended. These, unfortunately, have not been forthcoming. If the latest sociological studies on Catholic schools are any indication, the ability of these schools to orientate Catholics to the existential problems of our day (race, war and peace, poverty, etc.) has been a dismal failure. What comes through in these studies is the fact that such Catholics do *know* (intellectually) their Catholic dogma and fare better in institutional Church practices, such as Sunday Mass attendance, meat on Fridays, etc., than those Catholics who have not attended parochial schools in the United States. Yet, this performance pinpoints the agony of the Catholic school, for this is the kind of behavior which is making Catholicism largely irrelevant in our society. It encourages the already prevalent parochialism, ghettoism, and concern only with institutional structures, instead of with the interests of the larger community of men. It would be far better for the Church to divert its talents and resources away from such sources of ghettoism and into the mainstream problems of the age.

All this leads these excellent priests to an almost complete despair in the present structural organization of the Church. After suffering much to change it and seeing that they simply cannot or that its leaders prefer "prudence" so as not "to disturb the faithful," they simply opt for out and try to lead as Christian an existence as they can, some of them with a woman they can love and who will love in return. It is not the woman here who is the source of the difficulty but the structural organization of the Church and its unwillingness or inability to innovate radical change. Marriage is, in these cases, not the cause of their leaving but the end result, in order thereby to establish the loving Christian community which they did not find in the Church.

Unfortunately, the attitude of the layman toward the priest is usually one of ambivalence, and even when it is not, the priest is put on a sort of pedestal above the average needs of men. In fact, he is made to be a super-man. In reality, he is perfectly a man like all the rest and even, because of his celibacy, has a greater emotional need to be loved and appreciated. This is a point of obligation which the Catholic community has totally neglected in its relationship to its priests. If it wants to keep a celibate priesthood, it is under the obligation to support the priest emotionally *by its love* and acceptance. Only then can he, in his turn, be the eschatological witness to the other kingdom among men (the very *raison d'être* of the charism of celibacy). In reality, the Catholic community has not been community to him, but a "parish" which asked of him his "services" and left it at that because that is the way the present Church is structured and organized. The community itself does not know *how* to love outside of the specifically sexual domain which is the family. They are ignorant of what love (New Testament *agape*) can mean in context of the larger family of the Christian community or of all mankind. The terrible result is that there is no community; nationalism, super-patriotism, racism, chauvinism, and other narrowing socio-logical *cadres* can "co-exist" in the Christian who by his vocation is Catholic and universal.

When the secular clergy claim the right to marry, it is not—as is often thought in lay and clerical circles—that the "burden is too heavy" or that they are under the illusion that they will get rid of their present problems through marriage. There may be a few who think this way, but usually such persons should never have become priests in the first place and probably would not have made good husbands and fathers as well. Such accusations only serve to obscure the real issue, which is an existential priestly living and consecrating of the terrestrial realities of concrete familial existence—one of the most fundamental drives of human nature. The real "problem" is that the secular clergy do not know (in the biblical sense of the word) the concrete problems of their people. This incarnational dimension of the ministerial priesthood was lived for hundreds of years and in no way took away from the charismatic and eschatological witness of monks and nuns. But it was lived as another experience, one with the whole people in the world.

It is also evident that, in the *Constitution on the Church in the Modern World,* both anthropology and Christology are intimately related and connected (par. 45). As a matter of fact, in the present order of creation-redemption, they are absolutely inseparable. Man and his history in all of its ramifications becomes intelligible only in Christ, for He alone gives man the final direction of His own mystery in time. The Incarnation of the Son of God has destroyed forever the notion of a temporal human existence, a neo-

Platonic spirituality existing outside the basic structures of man's earthly existence. The Incarnation has brought man himself an understanding of his historical existence, as well as its fulfillment. In Christ, in the words of St. Irenaeus we have all been "recapitulated" and it is in Him that we find the meaning of our historical existence on earth. Man is the microcosm of the universe according to the Greek Fathers; but now, in Christ, he joins both heaven and earth, the terrestrial as well as the celestial city. It is then a Christology which must guide our Christian anthropology, which, in fact, is exactly what the *Constitution* does. This is all the more reason why we must have knowledge of man himself in the totality of his earthly commitment, that is, in his economic, social, cultural, physiological, and political aspects. If we would understand man, then we cannot neglect any of these aspects of man's existence.

The secular (from the Latin *saeculum,* pertaining to the world) priesthood is a living witness to these incarnational dimensions of the Church, among which is the most important, namely, that of marriage and family. This can also serve to justify the existence within the Church of both a married and a celibate clergy as long as celibacy remains what it is: the charismatic eschatological calling by God to a particular individual (not necessarily a priest), never imposed by positive ecclesiastical law.

Does all this advance the argument for a married clergy? The vast majority of the clergy with whom I am acquainted feel exactly this way and some are even willing to act as "signs" to the Church by leaving, thus creating a shock for a possible future correction of this situation. But this solves nothing since Church leaders are thereby confirmed in their view that these few only were the *malcontents* without whom the Church is better off. The future—at least for the moment—does not look promising. What small steps have been taken once again lay bare the terrible dishonesty in the Church when facing this great problem. In 1963, permission from Rome was granted to bishops to bring back to the fold those priests who had left but who were old or who had families they could not give up. Later, such permission was to be given to all who had left and married. The consequent absurdity is that if a priest wanted to marry, there was no way for him to leave in good standing, but if he "sinned" he could then be "fixed up." Finally, this permission was given and is given to those who apply, but this was and is to be kept secret so as "not to scandalize" the faithful or so that Rome does not get a flood of requests. This in itself is a terrible indictment of a mentality that actually believes the majority of priests remain priests not because they love the priesthood but because of fear and coercion. Perhaps the system has so wounded them that the Roman authorities are quite right, but this itself cries to heaven for immediate remedy. Needless to say, these men are thus "reduced to the lay state," that is, they are no longer permitted to exercise their priesthood. What shall we say of the pain and agony of those poor priests who left and were treated (and *are* treated) by the organized Church—clergy and people alike—as outcasts and criminals? Are there any words strong enough to condemn the heartless self-righteousness of many members of the organized Church who have so mistreated these poor men? Our immediate penance must be to find them at once, reinstate them as laymen or as married priests if they so wish, and find functions (which are by no means lacking in the Church today) for them to perform.

That the present discipline on celibacy will change is a foregone conclusion. It is not a question of *if* but *when,* since men today recognize that no one can take away the natural right of any man to marry. Much like the condemnation by Rome of religious freedom in the nineteenth century which became incorporated into the life of the

Church at Vatican II, we shall have to wait for a pope other than Paul VI to recognize the profundity of this problem. The most we can do now is to study the problem more deeply until another generation of authority will recognize what the secular world has long since seen in forcing priests to make such an agonizing decision. In this case, as in so many other tragic decisions of the past 500 years, the Church will be the follower, not the leader.

Smoke Screens and Sacred Cows

Archbishop
Thomas D. Roberts

ARCHBISHOP THOMAS D. ROBERTS, now in his middle seventies, is a Jesuit priest and former Archbishop of Bombay, India. He resigned his archbishopric (1937 to 1950) in order to expedite the appointment of a native Indian to the post. Since that time he has been an open critic of ecclesiastical authoritarianism, marriage courts, and birth-control policy. In 1964 he edited a collection of essays by ten Catholic authors in a book entitled Contraception and Holiness. *In the book's introduction he stated: "Thus far I have not been persuaded by any of the natural-law arguments against contraception. They do not seem to me to be conclusive, and if I were not a Catholic, I probably would feel obligated on the grounds of my own rational examination of the question to accept the viewpoint of the Lambeth Conference and of the large body of non-Catholic theologians and philosophers." At Vatican II he studiously avoided the speaker's rostrum, preferring to state his views at press conferences "which went out in twelve languages, and all the bishops read it who would otherwise have been either at the coffee bar or asleep." For many years Archbishop Roberts has been a courageous participant in disarmament efforts. He now lives in retirement in a Jesuit house in London.*

Readers of such reviews as *Informations Catholiques Internationales* find evidence in every number of the world-wide tension created by the treatment of certain practices as "sacred cows." Though merely disciplinary, not doctrinal, these have hitherto been regarded as fundamentals beyond all questioning.

To such categories belong the fact reported in August, 1965, that a major seminary in Brazil with 115 students run by the Lazarist (Vincentian) Fathers has been closed by its Archbishop pending the introduction of conciliar reforms. The demands of the students could no longer be ignored when 90 percent of them declared opposition to the law of clerical celibacy.

No doubt the vote at Vatican II in favor of allowing married deacons reflected recognition of such an attitude, and it made a beginning at the lower (but still major) level of the diaconate—no less apostolic in origin than the priesthood. On the basis of Jewish practice, it is as likely that the first six companions of St. Stephen were married as that the fellow-apostles of the first Pope were also married.

When, in the last session of Vatican II, an approach was made to pursue the question of clerical celibacy to its logical conclusion in view of the grave crisis of priestly vocations in some countries, Cardinal Tisserant announced in the Pope's name that the matter could not be discussed there and then; but he added that every conciliar father

was free to send in his views. It did not need to be added
that the laity could make their own appropriate contribution to this problem. It is their flesh and blood and spirit
that produce the priest, their money that educates him,
feeds and clothes him. Anyhow, if lay silence and passivity
on such an issue could be justified, it could not be enforced.
Printing has been discovered. The "Index" is no more.

My attention recently has been drawn to a book pub-
lished in England by Leslie Frewin, in America by John
Day (1966). Its title is *All I Could Never Be* by "Ex-Father
George Long."

My remarks on some of the causes of a breakdown of
clerical celibacy may as well center on this book, partly because it is accessible to the reader, partly because the
author was one of my chaplains when I was Bishop to the
British Forces in India and Southeast Asia during the war.
He was my guest at Archbishop's House, Bombay; we lived
under the same roof at Karachi; and I can testify that if
Father Long's account needs correction, it is only that he
fails (naturally and properly) to record some outstanding
services he rendered as a chaplain.

From his life story I have selected those features which
parallel my own experience of fifty-seven years as a Jesuit,
forty-one as a priest, twenty-nine as a bishop, diocesan and
military, and more than ever (paradoxically) in retirement.

Father Long's comments on priestly vocation I would put
under the heads of:

1. Freedom and maturity of choice
2. Professional training
3. Relations with authority

His problem was not primarily tied to that of celibacy,
but any priest finding himself in difficulties due to any one
of these three factors will be in a predicament that is tied to
the problem of celibacy.

Since in the Western Church celibacy is taken for granted as an integral part of the priesthood, seminarians tend to shut out feminine influences automatically, and by way of compensation (in the psychological meaning of the term) they often turn more toward their mothers than other young men. Mother is "safe" and her influence is considerable. This is not thought out consciously, but, nevertheless, it can sway the final choice.

Father Long records his early indecision: "I shied away from the prospect of leaving school and becoming involved with my father's business. In fact, I had very little idea of what I actually wanted to be. My mother had mentioned that, above all, she would like me to be a priest."

About this time, a young seminarian was invited to tea. "My mother was kind and gracious. Over strawberries and cream I listened to her many questions about the seminary and her gaiety was obvious after he had gone. Perhaps this, after all, was a solution to my vacillating thought about the future. To be a student for the priesthood would give me some sort of prestige among my friends. The wishes of everyone would be reconciled."

But still unsure, he suggested "having a shot at this art business." This brought a blunt reply from his father: "There's no money in that. Why don't you think over the idea of becoming a priest? It would make your mother very happy."

He registered at the Art School of Durham University, but "after eighteen months I told my mother I would go to the seminary. She was overjoyed and I was pleased at her evident relief and happiness. Unsure of my motives, I began my studies for the priesthood in September, 1921, at the age of twenty."

Not surprisingly, the recurrent doubts of the reality of his vocation, which had troubled him from the very day of his ordination, became more acute on his mother's death:

"Deeper merely than the loss of a beloved parent was the persistent knowledge that now I had no purpose in continuing as a priest. . . . My mother had been my 'sheet anchor' and now I was adrift, subject to vacillations and influences that should have had no part in a priest's thought."

Father Long is honest about the doubt that assailed him even before he received the tonsure: "It takes courage to give up and return to the world. . . . I thought of the loss of face, what people would say, how my mother would find it difficult to reconcile with her deepest hopes."

But when he was about to receive the sub-diaconate he sought out a professor. It must be pretty obvious even to a lay reader that when he revealed his doubts and asked for advice, he should have had firmer guidance.

He was perfectly candid: "My mother wanted me to be a priest and I hated the idea of getting a job. Not a very good motive, is it?"

Asked about girls, he admitted that he was attracted, but "It's something I've learnt to control. My real anxiety is that I know in my heart of hearts I simply haven't got the love for religion I should have."

He was advised that prayer would help him to overcome his unrest.

Recording his second serious sexual lapse some years after ordination he says: "It seemed as if my prayers and efforts were of no use. I became involved with a girl as soon as time, place, and circumstances were favorable. . . . I knew I had sinned and would have to confess. But how could I be sincere when I was looking forward to seeing her again? My only solution to this ill-fitting overcoat of the priesthood would be to resign."

The initial immaturity of his choice and the lack of adequate professional training were further complicated by his relations with authority.

He has a bitter—and all too typical—story to tell of rectors remote from their curates, whom they treated as delinquent schoolboys, and who, at the same time, failed to ensure that assistant priests were fully occupied with responsible work. This held good in parishes in both England and America, and in both countries the author experienced little genuinely paternal concern on the part of his immediate superior.

The bleakness of many rectories, indeed, can scarcely provide the same buttress for an insecurely founded vocation that a happy home life may for a non-Catholic minister.

When the stability and strength of a good marriage are lacking, there should be something equally positive so that celibacy is not felt merely as a deprivation.

It is certainly arguable that a priest belonging to a religious order has, as Father Long affirms, more scope for his talents, and that he is therefore more completely fulfilled. He undoubtedly has the advantage of a wider companionship than the average secular, and there is the possibility of a court of appeal from rector to provincial before the ultimate recourse to a bishop.

The friendship of other priests can offer the emotional satisfaction that many priests need, and this can relieve the pressures of celibacy. Loneliness should not be added to the demands of the unmarried state.

Not that a policy of clerical segregation is the answer. Indeed, at the beginning of a priest's life, and while he is a seminarian, he is likely to become more stable if he mixes with laymen. As increasing numbers of clerical students take degrees at "open" universities, using the seminary as a hostel, the firmness of their vocation will be tested more thoroughly before the final decision.

When mistakes are made—and no system of probation

can be 100 percent certain—the traditional disciplinary methods of ecclesiastical superiors have usually made bad worse.

Among cases known to me personally is that of Father A. He was a member of a religious order whose vocation had been taken for granted by a devout Catholic family. As time went on, during his novitiate, he frequently mentioned to superiors that he had difficulties about sex. Notwithstanding, he was ordained. He was a modest, cheerful young man, constantly joking, and no one believed him, but as it turned out, it was true. He left the order six years after his ordination.

His family was very shocked, but the order treated him well financially and individual members kept up with him. What is pathetic is that during the thirty years in which he conscientiously brought up a good Catholic family, neither he nor his wife could go to the Sacraments. An almost intolerable strain was placed on the marriage as a result, but somehow it survived.

Every effort was made on his behalf at Rome, but in vain. It was not until 1965, at the age of sixty-six, that he was allowed to marry in the Church.

Yet this was a man whose most intimate friends could see had a true vocation to marriage. He had felt compelled to give up his priesthood, but the last thing he wanted was to leave the Church. He was no rebel, no doubter. The only way open to him after his marriage, if he wished to be technically a "good Catholic," was to live in a brother-and-sister relationship with the woman he loved.

It proved impossible and he fathered four children. On top of these difficulties, there was the burden of his secret. Think, for example, of the daily questions of the children, the little things that could be answered casually in any other family. Why does a priest wear a funny collar? What sort of things do you have to tell in confession? Will you come to the school concert, Daddy?

For a number of years he and his wife waited for the question they knew was inevitable—"Why don't you and Mummy come to Communion with us?"

They had never been able to decide how they would tackle this, and then one day it came out of the blue from a little daughter who had inherited her father's directness.

Characteristically, he replied: "Because Daddy's been naughty." He was as humble as he was honest, and having told the children he had been a priest, he then incautiously let it slip in the convent, the girls' school.

The nuns no doubt believed that they practiced charity, but for all that, though the two girls were kept on at the school, from then on there were constant pricks to remind them that they were somehow outside the pale.

The strong faith in their home and the love that surrounded them brought them through, but they certainly shared their parents' trial. They had, at least, a reasonably comfortable home, for their father had taken a degree before ordination and was able to get a well-paid job. In this he was more fortunate than many men in a similar situation.

Father B had a degree too, but his temperament was very different. He was high strung and exceedingly self-conscious about his position.

He eked out a living correcting examination papers so that at least he did not have to face the outside world. He was always painfully and inescapably aware of his broken vows. He accepted that, by way of expiation, he must meet the commitment he had undertaken by his marriage of supporting his wife and child, but he also accepted the condition laid down by Rome of a brother-sister life.

The cramped flat in a near slum, which was all he could

afford, the lack of intellectual companionship (his wife was a very simple woman), and the feeling of guilt he was never able to shake off added up to a degree of unhappiness that few of us are called on to bear.

Father C, humanly speaking, finished up as a complete wreck. He was a diocesan priest with no paper qualifications or particular skills. A popular newspaper "featured" his registry office wedding and the house-trailer where he set up home, and the camera even followed him to his first job in a canning factory. The publicity evoked increased anger from his bishop, fellow-priests, and the laity of the district.

But there was no camera to record the shutdown of the factory when he lost his job, nor his wife's subsequent walkout, nor the end of the road when he became an alcoholic.

The case of Father D was brought to my notice during the Vatican Council. He was a diocesan priest who had married in a civil ceremony. Both parties recognized very soon that they had made a mistake, even from the point of view of their own happiness. A prelate asked me if I could find an American bishop who would accept him in his diocese. One bishop told me—inaccurately, as it proved—that no other American bishop would touch the case. Another did, in fact, offer to have him. He was a canonist and he told me that, had the priest wished to stay with the girl, it would have been easier now to get permission for them to be married properly in the Church than it would be to get a dispensation from the censure attached to the civil marriage of lay Catholics.

There have been a number of similar cases. In other countries marriages have been not infrequently contracted with the permission of the Holy See. One of the earliest that made headline news was of a priest in the Diocese of Versailles who was allowed by the Holy See to marry, but under promise of keeping the matter a profound secret.

After the marriage he thought better of the promise, extracted, as it seemed to him, under duress, and which, if kept, would prevent a large number of others with as good a title as his own from being freed from their vow.

It is this arbitrary imposition of secrecy, only abjured reluctantly in the last few months on the part of the Holy Office, which has done endless harm to the Church. It seems to be part of the old policy of treating the laity and junior clergy as infants in a school.

The hopeful element now is that in some places, as in Holland, the matter has been publicly discussed on television, even by the Cardinal Primate. In America, the freedom of information used by the newspapers and magazines such as *Commonweal, Jubilee,* and the *National Catholic Reporter* is forcing the Church to abandon smoke screens, which cloud the issue and stifle the voices of those who have a vital interest in the matter—priests themselves, and nuns, their parents and relatives, that whole Catholic body which *is* the Church.

Dutch priests, canvassing opinions (November, 1966) in connection with the meeting of the Dutch National Council (the subject was on their national agenda, though not discussed at the Council), were not concerned to hide their views. A statement signed by more than one hundred, including professors at the Catholic University of Nijmegen, as well as by parish priests and seminary lecturers, urged that celibacy should no longer be obligatory for ordination to the priesthood.

The signatories claimed that though celibacy can be a blessing for the Catholic community and for priests themselves, the well-being of the Church and its ministers' personal happiness are damaged by the juridical obligation of celibacy; that this keeps some away from the priesthood and makes others, often good and capable pastors, lay down their office.

A public-opinion poll conducted by Attwood Statistics gives 77 percent of all Dutch people in favor of a married clergy, and 57 percent of Dutch Catholics.

Some of the cases referred to me raise the same doubts in my mind as have recently been expressed by theologians and canonists on the necessity of giving far more importance to human rights, even to the revision—already promised—of Canon Law.

One particularly unhappy priest had brought his case to the diocesan court preparatory to reference to the Holy See. His evidence for the invalidity of his ordination on the grounds of excessive outside pressure and of immaturity seemed to me quite as strong as some of the evidence on which Roman courts have nullified a marriage. But the impression was given of a perfunctory judgment, the consideration of a case of which the failure was predetermined.

Yet to annul a marriage is to touch a bond of divine origin; the law of celibacy, on the other hand, is of human origin, as the history of the early Church proves.

Such cases, and many others, seem to have produced an authoritative policy, the same sort of closed mind which a sexual question tends all too easily to produce in fallen human beings. In any other department of human life the same degree of callousness to human suffering, the same tendency to turn into absolutes values those which are only relative, would be unthinkable. The remedy can only be in a more Christian attitude, in effective communication between a celibate priest and hierarchical authority at one end, and the Catholic people of God at the other.

Too frequently after tragedies have occurred (often traceable to poor professional training which took no account of the difficulties a priest would encounter) the bishop or superior has said, in effect, "If this man lets go of the rope, then he must drown."

When a priest goes to ask to be laicized, he is likely to

meet with less understanding and kindness than if his problem were drink, debts, or shaken faith.

If his reply to the question, "Is it a woman?" has to be
"Yes," he must be prepared for an emotional reaction of fear
or hostility; at best, often, puzzlement.

Yet, he might never have reached such a pass had his
training been different. The emphasis ought to have been
on preaching the Gospel, with celibacy being an aid to that,
instead of something necessary in itself, thereby looming al-
together too large in the priest's life.

"Good" women, too, can create havoc which the student
is not sufficiently prepared for. With a vague notion that a
priest is "different," pious Children of Mary will flirt, without adverting to the fact that they are, in fact, doing that. I
once heard a member of a woman's guild, asked about who
had taken a particular key, say: "No, it wasn't a man; it was
a priest."

Educated themselves to fear sex, it is not surprising that
many superiors have reacted with a horror that is anything
but helpful when they find their subjects in difficulty. Now,
however, there is a change for the better in this respect.

Oddly, the laity are often setting the pace and proving
more understanding and compassionate than senior clergy.
When an article on "fallen" priests was published recently
in a Catholic newspaper, a bishop protested and a parish
priest burned one hundred copies of the paper. Both gave
as their reason for disapproval the view that dissemination
of such facts would "scandalize the faithful." Yet not one
objection was received from a lay person, and, unasked,
hundreds of pounds were sent in to further the work of re-
habilitation which had been described.

Pope John, characteristically, found a gentle name for
priests who fail to keep their vows; he called them "shepherds in the mist." (Undoubtedly inspired by *Shepherds in
the Mist*, a book written by the late E. Boyd Barrett, a

former Jesuit priest who married.) A new attitude to such situations today is increasingly prevalent.

The roots of the old attitude are deep in the same sexual attitudes which are causing such bitter suffering to millions of Catholics all over the world in their marital relationships (think of the contraceptive issue, for example); causing a huge leakage from the Church, the greater part of it probably underground; creating possibly the greatest practical obstacle to effective relations between Catholics and Protestants.

The stock advice to priests under stress used to be prayer and the Sacraments—almost used as magic words to take the place of thought and treatment. These are needed, but certainly are not sufficient.

The question of a change in the law and of a completely new attitude toward sex involves open-mindedness in the conclusions to be reached. It also needs immensely greater emphasis on history in theological seminaries so that a priest can really form an adequate judgment in the development of thought about sex in the Church.

An illustration of the lopsided attitude toward sex has been the attitude toward married Anglican and other ministers who have gone over to Rome.

Each of these has contracted a solemn obligation equally sacred to all Christians to provide for his wife and family—in his case, through his ministry. If he comes to consider accepting the modern papacy as a serious obligation, an obligation in conscience, he will be told that he will lose his means of livelihood at an age when it probably would be very difficult or impossible to find another job. After years in the ministry, he then joins a laity with what may seem to him a very second-class citizenship.

Have we not implicitly put against a divine obligation (acceptance of Rome) a human obligation of refraining from the ministry simply because of marriage? His case will be all the worse if he knows the history of married clergy in the early Church and the radically different attitude—equally traditional—in the Orthodox Church.

There the priestly ministry and clerical celibacy are recognized for the two completely different vocations which in fact they are.

The practical difficulties are no doubt great, but it seems very hard to justify confinement to Germany and Holland of American priests ordained with full permission of the Holy See. But, thank God, American Catholics are growing up very fast.

I have found, often, that where lay people react strongly to the idea of a married clergy, the first comment is: "I could never go to confession to a married priest."

Such people have been amazed to learn of the ancient distinction between "Massing priest" and confessors—a distinction still observed in practice (of necessity) in many rural places in the East.

The average Eastern country priest does not lead a life apart from his flock in the same way that a Westerner does. He and his wife and children share the same sort of life; he is not noticeably superior to them either socially or financially, nor very much better educated.

There is not the Western tradition of frequent confession, so that there is no difficulty about a confessor from a monastery administering the Sacrament of Penance when he visits, sometimes only two or three times a year.

Now that the ice of Trent is cracking, Catholics are becoming willing to examine old disciplines in the light of modern conditions, and are more aware of the difference between discipline and doctrine. Mass on Sunday, fish on Friday, celibate priests, though on very different levels, have too often in the past been thought of as vital and permanent. In particular places, and at particular times, all these have been conducive to enrichment of the faith. But none of them is basic.

This is not a plea for a married clergy, but for the open-mindedness needed by an adult Christian to the treatment of an important issue.

Failures at "The Top"

Ruud J. Bunnik

RUUD J. BUNNIK, thirty-five, studied for the priesthood at the seminaries of the Archdiocese of Utrecht, The Netherlands. Following his ordination in 1957 he went to Nijmegen University to study English language and literature. After taking his master's degree in 1964, he was appointed to the faculty of the junior seminary in Apeldoorn. Since that time he has published regularly in Dutch periodicals, on the priesthood, priestly training, and especially on clerical celibacy. One of his longer articles, "The Question of Married Priests," was translated into English and published in Cross Currents *(fall, 1965, and winter, 1966). At the symposium on clerical celibacy, sponsored by the National Association for Pastoral Renewal (Notre Dame University, September, 1967), he read a paper on "Theology and Celibacy." In the fall of 1967 he published a book (in Dutch) entitled* Servants of the Aggiornamento, *a sketch for a renewed theology of the ecclesiastical ministry, taking into account the constitutions and decrees of Vatican Council II. English and Spanish translations of this book are in preparation. He was among the nine Dutch priests who, in 1966, asked their fellow Netherlands priests to sign a statement declaring that it was an urgent task for the Church to make celibacy optional for the secular clergy. The statement was signed by approximately one-third of the Dutch priests active in the pastoral ministry.*

During the years of preparation for the Second Vatican Council, more or less playful remarks could be heard about the golden era that was opening up for the clergy—the council was going to abrogate the law of celibacy. There was not a single indication that this was actually going to happen, yet those who expected a discussion on it were being reasonable. There was every logical reason to suppose that a problem which vexed so many bishops and priests would be put on the agenda.

Priests and candidates for ordination who had let themselves be seduced into some form of wishful thinking have been very much disappointed. On the whole the council did not pay much attention to them, let alone to their existential problems. The seminarist will perhaps find some comfort in the thought that a decree, and a not too bad one at that, has been drawn up for his superiors; at best, the priest will read the decree about "Priestly Work and Life" once and once only and then let it join the long row of devout but hardly inspiring publications on his bookshelf.

That the council and now the Pope have dashed superficial optimism to the ground is hardly a reason for distress; legislation so old and so strenuously defended cannot be put aside with one stroke of the pen. But more has happened. In nearly all assessments of the council's results complaints are heard that the problem of celibacy has been left unsolved. So there was a real problem. Some people kindly try to find an excuse for this, explaining that the matter was not yet ripe for a thorough discussion, or that it had not been given a place on the agenda. Explanations of this kind are not completely untrue, but they cannot be said to be real excuses. For it must be admitted that studies necessary for a thorough discussion have never been stimulated, but were, on the contrary, obstructed or dissuaded. And it is also true that even before the start of the council, requests for a discussion were handed in, in some cases by the bishops themselves. One is therefore justified in asking whether it was correct to keep celibacy off the agenda.

There is even more to be said: the present situation is absurd and paradoxical. If the subject had really not been on the agenda, or if during the deliberations it had become clear that no decisions could be made and the subject had been sent back for further study, it would have been possible to be reconciled. One could only have concluded that there was a failure in congressional technique, a failure that might have been prevented if the bishops had been given a real right to prepare the agenda.

But reading the reports of the meetings and studying the decrees that were put to the vote, one sees that celibacy was obviously an item of the agenda, and that real decisions have been taken. To be sure, there has not been a discussion about whether the law should be modified; it was decided that it should be continued without alterations. Moreover, a law of celibacy has been passed for the diaconate.

Of a council that has created such an absurd situation it is not sufficient to say that "it is a pity it did not tackle a difficult problem." Made without sufficient discussion, its decisions indicate a serious abrogation of pastoral responsibility.

A short survey of the events before and since the council and an analysis of the motives and arguments may help to clarify and evaluate the circumstances that confront us now. We must look not only at the priesthood, but also at the diaconate, because in the discussions about the latter not only did a correct view of the real issues seem to emerge, but also the first mistakes were made.

Sincere concern about the shortage of priests generated the demand for a renewed diaconate. The sometimes moving appeals made by bishops from regions with an extreme shortage managed to convince those who at first tended to shrink from this experiment; in the second session, on October 30, 1963, 75 percent of all bishops were willing to use this means of increasing the number of ecclesiastical ministers.

We cannot discuss here at length the merits of this decision—and it might well be inadvisable until experimental data have shown how the new diaconate works. All the same, one feels justified in asking whether, before deciding in favor of the diaconate, the council should not have spoken about possible means to remove obstacles to the priesthood. The diaconate is obviously an emergency measure. It seems clear that, in all future instances where a deacon will be appointed, a priest would have been even more useful. That the reintroduction of the diaconate was a rather impulsive decision may also be inferred from the fact that *Lumen Gentium* does not very satisfactorily define the tasks of a deacon. It even raises the suspicion that functions are being unduly clericalized that have long since been performed by lay people.

Council discussions revealed that among those opposing the diaconate were several bishops concerned about the preservation of celibacy. They had received the impression that married people, too, would be called to this ministry, and that this change would put an end to an age-long tradition of exclusively unmarried clergy. They wanted to prevent such a change. In order to avoid this mixing-up of motives it was decided to split the question. Thus a clearer answer would be possible as to whether the bishops were in favor of a renewed diaconate as such. On September 28, 1964, there were 1,903 affirmative votes, and the opposition had dwindled to a mere 242. In two additional votings the state of life of the future deacons was decided upon. With 1,598 votes for and 629 against, it was resolved that, if necessary, married people of a more mature age might be ordained deacons. A proposal to leave the unmarried deacon free to change his state of life by marrying was supported by 839 bishops; 1,364 bishops objected.

There is every reason to approve of the decision to vote separately on the new diaconate as a matter of principle. But some objections can be made against the two other votes, because the suppositions on which they were based are by no means unimpeachable.

First of all, *it is not absolutely clear that ecclesiastical authorities have a right to prescribe the state of life of the ministers.* Such a competence has never been claimed with regard to the laity, and there is general agreement that it does not, in fact, exist, although it may never have been explicitly stated. But does this mean that there is such a competence with regard to the ecclesiastical minister? Should not this have been proved first, especially in this case of a new form of ministry? The council took it for granted.

It also took something else for granted. Without any proof or comment it acted on the presumption that for this new ministry unmarried life is the ideal. This may be true, but no theological studies had been made on the matter, nor were there practical arguments based on experience.

These two *a priori* set the scene for the voting procedure. In this vote the bishops had to answer the following question: Which is more important, the shortage of ministers or an unproved ideal of celibacy? To what degree did the bishops think that the lack of ministers was forcing a partial renunciation of this "ideal" of celibacy? The results of the vote gave the answer: 1,598 bishops were willing to admit married deacons in emergency cases, but 1,364 so firmly believed in the unproved ideal of celibate deacons that they introduced a new law of celibacy for the unmarried deacon. Properly speaking, they introduced this law for all deacons, for it does not seem very likely that the married deacon whose wife dies will be allowed to contract a new marriage.

The bishops of Vatican II introduced a new form of celibacy and approved a scale of values in which a hypothetical ideal of celibacy won out over the much more evident need for ministers: celibacy, apparently, is more important than the needs of the faithful. What caused this pastoral failure? Either too few bishops realized that the recruitment of a sufficient number of deacons should be their first concern, or too many were plagued by a misguided fear of a frontal attack on priestly celibacy.

In the future, there will be married deacons and celibate ones, and they will do their own pastoral work. But when an unmarried minister wants to marry he will be declared unfit for further ministerial activity. The same dilemma has already cropped up for many a priest: he must either let his love for the ministry prevail, and, against the longing of his heart, work himself up to a heroic continence, or he must let his human heart speak out and leave the ministry, which will hardly be less painful.

The council has not only taken a decision which, from the point of view of pastoral care, is subject to doubt; it has also created a disciplinary situation that can lead to much human suffering.

In their discussions on the diaconate the bishops gave a negative answer to the question whether the demand for deacons was more important than the "ideal" of a celibate clergy. It could be expected that the same theme would be heard in the discussions on the priesthood, as the bishops surely anticipated. And if they did not realize it independently, others drew their attention to it. At least two memoranda on the subject were handed in at the beginning of the fourth session.

The first memorandum was written by a council *"peritus."* In an introductory section the author says that the old rule forbidding an ordained minister to marry should be kept. We cannot here criticize this point of view extensively, but can only remark that it is far from evident why this should be necessary, and that a continuation of this rule means that a real solution remains impossible for the minister whose celibacy has become a senseless burden, but who wishes to continue his ministerial activity.

The great merit of this memorandum lies in the fact that it frankly tells the bishops that they must consider the right order of precedence and must ask themselves if the traditional ecclesiastical preference for unmarried ministers does not seriously hinder them in carrying out their task to provide a sufficient number of priests. The author here refers to the decree on "Training for the Priesthood"—not yet put to the final vote at the time—which declares:

> The Shepherd and Guardian of our souls has constituted his Church in such a way that His Elect People must always and until the end of time have its priests, so that the Christian people be never a flock without a shepherd (Matt. 9:36). This will of their Master the apostles have understood, and therefore, they have, led by the Holy Spirit (Acts 13:2), reckoned it their duty to appoint ministers "who will be able to teach others" (II Tim. 2:2).

The present legislation of the Western Church, the author continues, starts from the assumption that married persons can hardly be of any use to the ministry. But this thesis is supported by practical arguments only, and is the outcome of a long historical development; it is, moreover, not accepted by the Eastern Churches, which cannot find a conclusive argument for it in Scripture, nor was it generally accepted in the Western Church up to the eighth century. By deciding to maintain this "standard of fitness," the bishops would not only hamper the recruitment of ministers, but they would also, and with insufficient justification, expect that from now on God will grant a sufficient number of cases in which vocation to the ministry and call to a celibate life coincide. The author therefore asks the bishops to consider seriously whether this "optimism" is warranted, and he reminds them that they themselves did not dare to start from this hypothesis in the matter of the diaconate. And, he finally asks, why do the bishops seem to make celibacy only, and not evangelical poverty as well, a *conditio sine qua non* for the ministry?

Not a single indication can be found in the decree on the priesthood that the considerations of this memorandum were given serious attention.

More or less the same lot fell to a memorandum which in the beginning of 1965 had been drawn up by the Dutch Catholic Society for the "Promotion of Mental Health." In four translations, and with the signatures of eighty-one well-known Catholic lay people from twelve different countries, this text was offered to the bishops shortly before the discussions on the priests-scheme started.

In this memorandum, the problem of celibacy is approached mainly from the point of view of anthropology and psychology. When the council, which is evidently prepared to revise pastoral activity with the help of a contemporary Christian anthropology, persists in an automatic linking-up of priesthood and unmarried life, it contradicts itself; such an attitude can no longer adequately exemplify the Church's relation to the world, nor does it agree with the generally accepted ideas of the rights of man. In point of fact this linkage often causes serious personal problems.

Thus it aggravates the shortage of priests in two ways: on the one hand it makes people leave the ministry; on the other, there is not the slightest doubt that many candidates, and very valuable ones at that, shrink from offering themselves for ordination because they are afraid they cannot accept the obligation to remain unmarried.

The people who drew up this text were aware of the fact that the council could not reasonably be expected to make radical changes on short notice. Therefore, the memorandum asked for the setting up of a post-conciliar commission to make further studies of the links between celibacy and the pastoral ministry. In doing this the council would show it was aware of the problems; it could also be expected that it would abstain from passing definitive pronouncements. This serious request was not listened to either.

The draft for a decree on the priesthood, which was given to the bishops in the third session, was judged unworthy of serious discussion. Therefore a new text was made and was discussed on October 13–18 and 24–26, 1965.

But on October 11th, before the discussions started, came the famous letter from the Pope. According to the conciliar procedures the bishops had to hand in the texts of their interventions a few days before, and from several texts it appeared that a serious discussion of the paragraph on celibacy was wanted. The exact wording and motivation of this demand cannot be ascertained, but something can be inferred from the intended intervention by Bishop Koop, whose text became public. He did not advocate a complete abrogation of the law, but only asked for such modification as would make it possible to have a married clergy as well as a celibate one; the main argument for his proposal was the alarming shortage in South America.

The fact that Bishop Koop was asked by several authorities to withdraw his text justifies the conclusion that it was his that was considered the most "dangerous." One may also suppose that his intervention was the direct reason for the Pope's letter, a letter addressed to Cardinal Tisserant and read out in the aula, in which the Pope not only declared that in his opinion a public discussion on celibacy was absolutely inopportune, but also that he himself was quite determined to uphold the law with all possible energy.

The bishops applauded. In the debates the word celibacy was hardly heard, and only one or two frank bishops are known to have made use of their right to intervene on the subject. In the decree that was passed the bishops voted to continue the legislation on celibacy, although they recognized that there was no necessary connection between ministry and celibacy and addressed a few friendly words to the "meritorious married priests" in the Uniate Eastern Church.

Anyone who now feels the need to ask critical questions about priestly celibacy is confronted with a firm personal opinion of the Pope himself; a conciliar decree which, passed with 2,243 against 11 votes, approves of the continuation of the present discipline; and, most lately, an encyclical.

The outlook for the future is none too bright. Even those who had not expected immediate radical changes felt disappointment, expressed in either resignation or vehement complaints about lack of realism and imagination, about neglect of duty and harshness, incompetence and narrowminded fear. The exodus from the ministry has not been halted. On the contrary, the most recent information suggests an increase in numbers. That there is much uncertainty about the exact numbers does not alter the case; if it is true that the official numbers are less alarming it will be useful to have them published as soon as possible. Meanwhile, the feelings of uncertainty among seminarians grow stronger; a ministry to which an increasingly number of people say farewell loses its attractiveness.

If this trend continues in the next few decades it is to be feared that before long there will be a disastrous shortage of younger clergy. In our changing times there must always be uncertainty about the ecclesiastical ministry, and the law of celibacy worsens the situation.

We cannot, therefore, be reconciled to the conciliar shortcomings. The serious study of celibacy must go on.

The massive "aye" which the bishops gave to the decree on "Priestly Work and Life" suggests a degree of *certitude*, though in fact it did not represent an unqualified approval and enthusiasm. But it was morally impossible to reject the text again; this would have been an even greater disgrace. So the text had to be carried through.

Still further, it may be said that the paragraph on celibacy does not reflect a well-considered and reasoned-out opinion of the bishops. For there was no room for a real discussion, and the very fact that the Pope decided to interfere shows that he was afraid of such a discussion. But why this fear? Is the Church really in danger when her discipline is reconsidered critically? The least we can say is that in this case we were subject to an unattractive disregard of the principle of collegiality, a principle that had been accepted less than a year before. What is this atmosphere of taboos? What is the real value of the bishops' vote?

It is difficult to imagine that the bishops were not really concerned about the situation. If there is any group of persons who know the exact facts, it is the bishops, and in their intensive encounters during the council they must have discussed the problem of celibacy. Nevertheless, they applauded after the Pope's letter was read, and this has disappointed many people. Was there, after all, a lack of understanding and an insufficient evaluation of the facts? It would seem that the answer to this question must be affirmative.

The difference between generations may have played its role. Most of the bishops are of advanced age. That does not make them unfit for their tasks, for "the Spirit blows where it wills," and a burden of years can go together with a great treasure of deep wisdom. All the same, it remains true that those bishops' sensitivity to many things, and especially vital things like sex and freedom, is different from that of many of the younger lay people and priests. Has sufficient account been taken of this fact? Has the opinion which the bishops laid down in their vote been formed in dialogue with the priests and the faithful of their dioceses? Or were the discussions and votings *"sur vous, pour vous, mais sans vous"*?

One is also inclined to think that many bishops did not realize that the problem of celibacy is not merely a problem for the individual priest, but that it is, first of all, a structure-problem of the Church. For many of them the law of celibacy is impregnable and not open to question. Starting from this hypothesis—that the legislation does rightly exist—they can see only two possibilities for a priest who is in trouble: either his wavering belief in his fitness for unmarried life is restored and he gives up the idea of marrying and remains in the ministry; or this belief does not return, and the priest becomes a "failure," no longer of any use for the ministry. Either decision causes pain, and no bishop, however great the paternal compassion, can alleviate it. But the bishop himself is hardly a less tragic figure. He will be saddened by the pain he must inevitably inflict upon another human being; moreover, he will be sorry to see his priests leaving.

Now the remarkable and even disquieting thing about all this is that many a bishop seems to be resigned to the situation. He can understand that a person is unable to live up to the "ideal," and he will ask the faithful to try to understand this. He does well not to ask their mercy, for this word suggests guilt, and this is not necessarily the case. But such a bishop does not seem to wonder whether a law, which in so many cases causes suffering that cannot really be healed, can justifiably be looked upon as being irreversible. But should he not do this? Should he not have the courage to ask if the dilemma "ministry-or-marriage" rightly exists? If, together with his fellow bishops of Vatican II, he has declared that there is no necessary link between priesthood and celibacy, should he not wonder whether he can support a law which says that it is impossible and sinful to marry after ordination?

Those are the questions about celibacy as a structural problem. And the fact that Vatican II ignored them constituted its great pastoral failure.

All these facts and considerations will have made it clear that we cannot completely agree with the Pope and the bishops when they say that celibacy was too delicate a matter to be given a public discussion. There is some truth in this, of course; nothing is gained by an exhibition of the human sufferings caused by the law of celibacy. But it is equally true that celibacy itself is part of the Church's public order, a law that is known to everyone, and that, besides, the shortage of priests, which is at least partly due to celibacy, is a public fact which can be illustrated with figures. No doubt it was the Pope's honest intention to prevent a pathetic evocation of human misery in the aula; but his letter also imposed silence on Bishop Koop and others who wanted a discussion on celibacy as a structural problem. Have we here another case in which "fear-inspired remedy was worse than the disease itself"? Problems are not solved by ignoring them. A Church in state of *aggiornamento* may, can, and must discuss its structural problems, especially when those structures are so apt to cause human suffering as is the case here. Is the optional biblical advice to those "who are able to receive this" really so much more important than "preach the Gospel to all people" and "do not impose burdens hard to bear"?

Studies and discussions must go on, if necessary, even without explicit invitation or approval from the Pope and the bishops; one may hope that the conciliar decisions will not be used as a means to repress those studies and discussions.

Why would it not be possible to break the deadlock on the local level? Until now the following question has hardly been asked, but it is high time to do so: Why must the whole Western Church have a uniform legislation on celibacy? In the field of practical government there has never been a complete uniformity in Christian life, and Vatican II itself has opened ways to further pluriformity. One need only look around: the liturgical reforms and the unequal introduction of them are leading to a variegated pattern of worship; different countries have different holy days of obligation; and even within a single ecclesiastical province mixed marriages are dealt with in different ways.

Even now there are already different legislations on celibacy within one Church: priests in the East and priests in the West, Latin priests and Latin deacons. Why couldn't local circumstances lead to a further differentiation? When East and West were reunited, their own traditions and the particular situation of the East were taken into account. Cannot part of the Western Church claim a similar right to let the local situation have a say? In an interview in Rome on November 10, 1965, Cardinal Alfrink seemed to envisage the possibility of differentiation:

> . . . it should not be forgotten either that the problem is not the same everywhere. Moreover, the reasons why a

differentiation is thought desirable may be quite different
in the various parts of the world . . .

In his letter to Cardinal Tisserant Pope Paul had shown
his determination to uphold the law and to give new luster
and strength to the ideal of priestly celibacy. The almost
complete lack of critical comment from the side of the
bishops—and from the side of the "great" theologians, who
so far have not seriously contributed to the discussion—and
the bishops' very affirmative voting on the decree on "Priestly Work and Life" must have convinced the Pope that his
line of policy was right. It could not reasonably be expected,
therefore, that his encyclical on celibacy (June 24, 1967)
would present a new approach or introduce any real changes.
Those who might have fostered this kind of unrealistic optimism had only to read the opening lines: "Priestly celibacy
has been guarded by the Church as a brilliant jewel in her
crown. . . ."

The encyclical is not a good piece of work. It is a monologue rather than a dialogue and does not realize what it set
out to do: to make the law of celibacy acceptable for those
who, for whatever reason, theological or practical, individual or general, doubted its pastoral justness. For we must
not forget the real issue in all present-day discussions: the
problem is not only and in the first place whether a celibate
priesthood is possible or desirable, it is also, and perhaps
even primarily, whether such an "ideal" of a celibate priesthood can be given concrete realization by means of legislation. Stating that priestly celibacy is beneficial to the
Church and to the individual priest is not enough; it must
be made clear that *obligatory* celibacy is good and useful.

Within the limits of this essay, I cannot give a detailed
critical comment on the encyclical and point out all instances where it has gone wrong. (This task is undertaken
elsewhere in this book.) But the following remarks may

show the bias of the whole text, and how many serious objections from the "opponents" are, sadly, ignored.

To start with, we must take a look at what the encyclical says about the unmarried state as such, about virginity "for the sake of the kingdom of heaven." Taken as a whole this is the best part of the Pope's letter; and we may add that a good and enthusiastic testimony in favor of virginity is by no means superfluous in our days, which tend to overestimate sex and to suggest that marriage is the central and ultimate value in human life. But this "defense" is overdone in at least two aspects. Celibate life is presented as a form of chastity, and even as a form of chastity superior to the chastity in married life. This is a serious flaw; for neither marriage nor celibacy is a form of chastity in itself: they are only ways of life which ask for a peculiar form of chastity, nothing else. Moreover, this kind of exaltation of celibacy can hardly escape depreciating marriage; not, of course, in a blunt way, but subtly, by suggesting that marriage is more in need of redemption than celibacy. "Jesus, in fact, has restored its original dignity, has honored it and has raised it to the dignity of a sacrament and of a mysterious symbol of his own union with the Church" (*n.* 20). All this may be true, but in the context of this encyclical it sounds condescending. The encyclical seems to forget that the bishops of Vatican II declined the use of the term "state of perfection" to describe religious and virginal life.

The second shortcoming is that the "permanency" of the unmarried state of life is taken for granted and in fact presented as a moral obligation. But is virginity of necessity permanent? Cannot this free charism and free choice be replaced and superseded by a new vocation, namely marriage? Cannot this become, for the individual, the "better way"? Present-day theology has only started studying this difficult question; the encyclical might have shown a little more reservation here.

The way in which the encyclical describes the priestly
ministry and the person of the priest is equally unsatis-
factory. It assumes that there is only one single and un-
changeable type of priest: full-time, exclusively engaged,
for life, in traditional parish work with a clearly defined set
of clerical activities, and with a strongly monastic spirituality. It seems unaware that at present there is much discussion going on about, *e.g.*, the fundamental distinction between layman and priest, about new forms of ministry (the
diaconate), about part-time priests, about the variability of
"priestly" spirituality, etc. The priestly image of *Sacerdotalis Caelibatus* is monolithic, petrified, and a-historical.
It is also supernaturalized. This priest is not an inhabitant
of the secular city and a member of the Church-in-this-
world, but a holy outsider, an incorporeal representative of
a hardly incarnated Christ, a man whose own physical existence hinders his work rather than serving as the touching-
point for his ministry. Maybe the encyclical is right in saying that for this type of priest celibacy is more or less natural
and desirable, but do these priests really exist, and do we
need them? And insofar as they do exist, they may be the
exception rather than the rule.

Accordingly, the encyclical cannot really admit that a
married priesthood could be a legitimate possibility. Of
course, it does not go as far as completely ignoring the first
ten centuries of the whole Church and the later history of
the Eastern Churches—the tradition of the Reformation
Churches is not even mentioned—and it repeats the words
of Vatican II that celibacy "is not demanded by the very
nature of the priesthood" (*n.* 20). But these traditions seem
to be marginal and not seen as an invitation to the Latin
Church to re-examine her own discipline. Nor can the encyclical admit that those who, within this Latin Church, are
asking for a renewed and thorough study may be led by the
Holy Spirit to do so. Several of their arguments are men-

tioned, but they are not answered seriously. Answers, given, for the most part are simplistic and in a few cases even unfair. To give only two instances.

1. The encyclical cannot believe that there is a real connection between the law of celibacy and the shortage of priests. Now every bishop and every seminary superior can testify that many a seminarian broke off his training because he felt unfit for unmarried life, and that many a priest has asked for laicization because he wanted to marry. Here the encyclical demonstrates a real blindness to the sober facts.

2. The encyclical refers to the "lamentable defections" (*n.* 83ff). Members of the Church will be properly concerned about the growing number of priests who leave the ministry, indicating a real crisis; but is it right to suggest that all who defect feel wretched and guilty because they have been too careless, have neglected their religious duties, and have chosen a way that God is sure to have disapproved? Such a suggestion not only ignores the fact that many former priests are really happy in their new state of life, but also the possibility that there could be a failure on the side of "the Church." This, to my mind, shows the basic bias of the whole encyclical. For the basic question is not whether there are good arguments in favor of a celibate priesthood, but whether the present discipline of obligatory celibacy has the support of *the whole Church*. The encyclical identifies the opinion of the Pope and many of the bishops with the opinion of the Church as a whole. Can this be maintained in the post-Vatican II era, especially in matters of practical discipline? Vatican II solemnly accepted the principle of collegiality and co-responsibility of all members of the people of God. Shouldn't this be applied here? Discussions and surveys in many countries have shown that many serious lay people and priests are asking for a change in the law. The kind of monologue

"from above" presented in the encyclical is not a real answer to these questions. Only in a patient dialogue and with a willingness to acknowledge that the Holy Spirit is working in *every* member of the Church shall we be able to discover where this Spirit is leading tomorrow's Church.

The disciplinary institutions of a living Church are not necessarily permanent. A renewed Church may ask for a change in the traditional law of celibacy. Therefore the discussion will go on. It must go on, even if Pope Paul, misled by the failing bishops of Vatican II and afraid to invite serious "critics" to help prepare an encyclical, would be worried about it. In spite of its serious shortcomings *Sacerdotalis Caelibatus* may provide a starting point. For it admits what has never been admitted before: that priestly celibacy and a law of celibacy are not self-evident and cannot be taken for granted. The months that have elapsed since the publication of this encyclical have already shown that the discussions will go on and become even more widespread. The National Association for Pastoral Renewal in the United States did not cancel its planned symposium, which was held at Notre Dame University in September, 1967. New inquiries have been set up, among them one officially sponsored by the bishops of The Netherlands. The stream of publications has become larger than ever before. It is not unthinkable that within a few years we shall be able to say that *Sacerdotalis Caelibatus,* instead of putting an end to all discussions and stopping the development, has in fact speeded them up and in this way has led to a quicker solution of a truly urgent problem.

At Vatican II and in Pope Paul's encyclical, "The Top" failed to discuss the matter realistically. Perhaps these pastoral failures can be mended from the bottom upward.

Committing Matrimony

Edward F. Henriques

THE REVEREND EDWARD FRANK HENRIQUES, forty-seven, is an ex-Roman Catholic priest (Franciscan). He prepared for the priesthood at the Franciscan Novitiate, San Luis Rey (California), and the Franciscan Theological Seminary, Santa Barbara (California). He was ordained June 10, 1945, and for sixteen years pursued a ministry remarkable for its diversity: high school teacher and principal at St. John's Indian school, Laveen (Arizona); parish priest at St. Francis Church, Sacramento (California); preacher of parish missions and retreats on the Franciscan "mission band" covering the entire Western United States; retreat master at Serra Retreat House, Malibu (California); Hour of St. Francis (TV) in Los Angeles; co-editor, Way magazine, a journal of religion, San Francisco. Shortly after his marriage he left the ministry, taught at Austin, Texas, public junior and senior high schools, taught Latin at Concordia College, Austin, and pursued further studies at the Episcopal Theological Seminary of the Southwest. In August, 1965, he was received into the Episcopal priesthood and served as priest-in-charge at St. Mark's Episcopal Church, Austin. On June 1, 1967 Father Henriques was appointed rector of St. Luke's Episcopal Church, Livingston (Texas), where he still serves. He resides at the parish house with his wife and children.

I am a damned Roman Catholic priest. Quite literally. Some would say metaphorically also. I am excommunicated, anathematized, damned because I committed matrimony. That did it. It wasn't any extra-parochial sexual dalliance or throttling my provincial—it was only the commission of marriage that consigned me to hell's fires.

When I left the Catholic priesthood, I was not excommunicated. I actually left with the blessing of Rome. (They were glad to be rid of me.) Laicized, I was: reduced to the lowly estate of a plain layman.

I had been a priest for sixteen years. But it had become a monstrous chore. Worse, I was wholeheartedly bored. But better, I had fallen hopelessly, ecstatically in love with the most wonderful woman in the world and had married her, although the provincial did not know this detail.

My good provincial—and he was good in his own little medieval way—was already a mite or more suspicious about my spiritual relationship with a particular woman. He had warned me paternally. I had listened filially—and limited my visits to daily.

My little medieval provincial didn't screech in horror, then, when I came to him requesting out. The petition would have to go to Rome, but in the meantime he could grant me temporary leave of absence. Good enough. Bless his heart, I knew that inwardly he was heaving a vast sigh of relief, for he was secretly afraid of a lurid scandal erupting into glaring headlines.

143

He reminded me, praise his thoughtfulness, that my vows of obedience and chastity remained in effect. This was sheer formality, for he knew—though he had never said so to me—that I had dispensed myself from chastity some years ago.

He said all the right things that day: all the spiritual and fatherly things expected of a provincial on such a dire occasion. I listened raptly.

The laicization request which I was to sign contained one easily-overlooked little phrase, "*Castitate semper servata,*" "Chastity being always observed." Good grief. Great show: I was free to leave the priesthood, but not to marry. I asked if the offending phrase might be deleted. Nay, nay. The request may not be presented without the obnoxious "celibacy rider."

But I sorely wanted that dispensation, for the sake of my saintly mother. My departure was going to be unthinkably painful for her, but this Roman dispensation would assuage the pain a good deal. (She was the sole reason I had not departed at leave five years previously; others could absorb the shock of my exit. She could not. It would pain her deeply, and I would have given my right arm to spare her this. But I would not have given my life and another's and I did not.) But I signed the laicization request, a meaningless gesture at the time.

We shook hands and I left. On my way out the provincial's secretary, also a priest, asked me if I needed any money to "get started." Alas, foolish pride. I politely declined, and within six weeks I was on the brink of starvation.

I did not look back as I walked from the provincial's office that day, nor did I look back a few hours later when I closed my rectory door behind me. My description here has been lightsome, but I had felt a huge, engulfing sadness at the bishop's office that morning. And again when I said goodbye to the priests in my parish rectory. These men had been my closest friends since seminary days. For more than twenty years we had studied and golfed, prayed and drunk whisky together. But as I headed my battered Chevy out of town I had only one glorious sensation: freedom!

Years have passed since that day and some of them have been rocky indeed. Not one of those years has been even half so serene as those of my priesthood. My wife and I were reduced to an alfalfa diet within four months. And it was as though I had just escaped from Leavenworth. In seeking employment, where had I been for those past sixteen years? On Mars? Ex-priest is still, I fear, a very dirty word in vast circles.

But I never longed for the halcyon, opulent days of the priesthood. My only regret was that I had dallied so long before departing. All those good youthful years wasted, squandered. Now I had rejoined the human race, and I lived and loved every minute of every day. And I still do.

This was what life was all about. This was the way God meant it to be. These have been the happiest years of my life. What I did was as right as sunlight, as God-inspired as any action ever perpetrated on this earth.

Isn't it obvious that marriage should fulfill and enlarge a man? It is platitudinous to say that an unmarried man is only half a man, but he's at least an anomaly. Usually. Thank God for the brilliant exceptions. You cannot beat nature, the way things are, the way God made us—this is one of the most basic tenets of Catholic philosophy. And what more basic than that He made us male and female? And how can you beat it? "A fellow needs a girl, his own kind of girl."

But the thousands and millions of unhappy marriages? The divorces, the marital hatred? Either she's not his own kind of girl, or one of them—sometimes both—refuses to grow up. Undoubtedly our marriage was exceptional: we were both forty years old when we vowed to love and to cherish from that day forward. I love my wife today more than I did on our wedding day. I know her better; I see more to love. God willing—and He is—I will love her even more by the time, far distant, when I come to die.

Did I mention the halcyon days of the priesthood? Long gone. And small wonder: the kids! But they're darling and precious. Watching them growing, trying, laughing, crying, playing, praying—can this be bad? Is this of Satan?

One slobbery kiss from my youngest, Billy, with his flashing black eyes is worth all the anguish and hard work. One whispered confidence from Linda makes up for all those nasty phone calls from those mean old people at the bank.

Quick as a flash my former priest-companions are going to accuse me of "rationalization" should they chance to read these words. I can scarcely blame them. I used the same term many times of other "apostate" priests. It's standard procedure. It's the stock answer we were all taught. I guess we all rationalize somewhat as we go through life, else we've deprived our very existence of validity. But here the roots go much deeper.

Marriage is the most profound, most elemental of all human relationships. If God fashioned human nature, He made marriage the manner of existence. Not simply a possible choice of vocation. But for the vast majority of mankind, the *way* in which one is to live, and be happy, and achieve salvation. Marriage is not a fringe-benefit, an accoutrement. It is of the very essence of life, what it is all about. Nothing on earth or above it can take the place of this elemental relationship.

Nuns sometimes have a very real, personal relationship to God. This relationship can be an exquisite thing: a virginal soul dedicated to her heavenly Spouse. Surely this attitude can be a very fulfilling substitute for married love, but it is still precisely that, a substitute. It is, perhaps, a higher, loftier thing—I don't know—but it still cannot take the place of conjugal love as the basic pattern of human life upon earth.

Many will have a simple explanation of my "defection" —*sex*. They've got something there. But not everything. That would be gross oversimplification. Sex there has been, will be, and aplenty, God strengthen us! A wise man once said, "If God made anything better, He kept it for Himself."

Even narrowly considered, sex is a very important element of marriage. Trouble is, it often *is* marriage. But it isn't a dirty word, and it isn't marriage. It should permeate and vivify marriage by day and by night, every moment of living. Sex isn't merely something that happens between married people in bed at night. It is the quintessence, the distilled essence of married love. The love is there twenty-four hours a day, and sometimes it simply cannot contain itself any longer and it overflows into sex.

I ask further: is it not significant that Canon Law imposes no punishment whatever upon such extra-parochial diversions as clerical fornication, adultery, sodomy, flagrant promiscuity, or any other form of sexual aberration, nor even for continued and prolonged concubinage, but only for "committing" matrimony? This is the unpardonable crime. How many times have I heard priests say—and for shame, I have said it myself—do what you will, but don't marry her!

Does it require an angel from heaven to prove to us that the law of clerical celibacy has been a dangerous law almost from its very inception? And history books will bear me out. I used to twit my priestly confreres, "Let's face it, gentlemen, the law of celibacy has never been a success." For some reason that remark never went over very well. I have the feeling that the law of celibacy has engendered more sexual deviation, more promiscuity, than it has ever fostered virtue.

The protests over what I have written here will be many and shrill. Some will appear cogent, but not to me. Immediately it will be said that I made a solemn promise before God and man to live a celibate life. That I did, and I was free and twenty-one. But I will stoutly maintain that a callow, idealistic, totally sheltered seminarian of twenty-five years has not the foggiest notion of what he is really being asked to forsake. How can he? Is it reasonable that an indoctrinated youth of twenty-five years should tell me, a weathered middle-aged man, how I should live the rest of my life? That young man of twenty-five years ago, green-as-green, is as far removed from the me of today as I am from Florence Nightingale—or Pope Paul VI.

I have written these words without bitterness or rancor—only complete conviction. I have no animosity toward the Church or my former priest-companions. Only compassion, really. Some are such fine men, but slaves to a relentless, antiquated code.

When I joined the ranks of the great unfrocked—I am told that there are some 10,000 of us souls in the U.S. today—I had hoped to retain the friendship of a few of my very closest priest-buddies. I was a bit naive. Today there is not a single Catholic priest whom I can call a friend. When I gracelessly departed they were pained and grieved; they felt that I had betrayed them. They had liked me personally, once, but now, according to the laws, I was a traitor. I had dared to do the one thing, the only thing one dare not do: marry. Here the system is inexorable.

If it is said that my argument is specious, so be it. If it is said that I exaggerate, I can only say that I do not. I have found happiness such as I never knew. I am a whole man, finally. Mother Church may regard me as *excommunicatus* or *vitandus* (to be avoided)—but God doesn't.

Out of Habit

Mercedes Alonso

MERCEDES ALONSO was educated at the University of Puerto Rico and DeSalle University School of Law. She also has studied journalism at The Catholic University of America. For more than twenty-five years she has worked closely with nuns in missionary and social work among the poor. She was a nun herself from 1948 to 1950. Miss Alonso is presently working as a technical assistant for a specialized agency of the United Nations. She is fluent in French, Spanish, and Portuguese. Her home is in Washington, D.C.

What are the forces and conflicts driving nuns to relinquish their convent vows after fifteen to thirty years in religious life?

Startling as it may sound, the steadily rising number of dedicated women who are daily leaving the convents is not creating the crisis but revealing it. At no time in the history of the Catholic Church has the concept of freedom, which today claims the whole world as its stage, penetrated the tightly sealed enclosure of convent life with more vigorous force. Public utterances by a few vocal nuns are appearing with more and more frequency in the Catholic as well as in the secular press and reflect a growing impatience with what they term "meaningless traditions and restrictions." Many of these restless and imaginative nuns, who for the present have chosen to remain, are said to be pressing for changes in their archaic Rule and environment. But as one sister puts it, "There is the constant fear of being labeled too liberal or rebellious and thus finding yourself ostracized by the decision-making conservative elite." Others, despairing of the slow pace of reform, if any, and disappointed by the betrayal of a dream, are coming out to enter the arena of social revolution, claiming that this can only be accomplished effectively outside the convent walls.

"The world is on the verge of a great spiritual renaissance," stated former Sister Jacqueline Grennan, in a nationwide television interview following her request to be released from her canonical vows. She is now lay president of Webster College.

"I don't know where this mood will lead but I feel it is going to lead to great and wonderful things." Sister Francetta, President Emeritus of Webster College, told me shortly after Miss Grennan announced that the college would be secularized. Sister Francetta, who hailed the announcement as "world-stirring news," is still a member of the Sisters of Loretto. Breaking from the cloister tradition, she went to live in an apartment in the Foggy Bottom section of Washington, D.C., while serving as assistant director of the Women's Job Corps Center.

Nuns are now openly acknowledging the exodus from their ranks. For the first time the Church has set up "quickie" administrative procedures to process applications of those who want to be released from their vows, which can now be done in the short space of four to six weeks and by means of a printed form instead of a letter. This is not to say that the Church has abandoned its orthodox position on the sacredness of religious vows. It does indicate, however, that the Church is taking a more realistic view and a more practical approach to the problems that plague religious life in a modern society of free men.

The points of controversy range from personal and intellectual freedoms, unquestioned obedience, primacy of conscience, human emotions, to the lack of reality in the nun's day-to-day life, often described as being in harsh contrast to its professed ends.

One middle-aged woman who was director of a school of nursing and who had spent twenty-nine years in religious life expresses it this way:

"In the name of obedience you are asked, by well-meaning but often erring superiors, to obey commands which fly in the face of common sense." She recounts how convent rules and regulations control even the most inconsequential act of a nun's everyday life: "A bottle of aspirin, for common use in every American household, is refused on the premise of possible abuse. Individual judgment is often denied, solely on the strength of the superior's own reasoning and many times with no reference to the realities of our time."

She recalls the incident which was mainly responsible for her final decision to leave the convent. On the contention that the Rule permits only one monthly letter home, she was refused permission to write to an unfortunate girl who had attempted suicide several times and who was obviously in need of a helping hand.

"I was gripped by the fear," she recalls, "that in blindly obeying the Rule I was becoming thoroughly impoverished in human emotions. I felt that I had to crack the shell of the conventional image, to permit the true person to emerge. I could no longer remain within the narrow limits which allow only enough room to exist."

Equally revealing are the remarks of another young woman who recently left the convent: "It is a supreme absurdity to attempt to solve the problems of the soul and of the intellect by administrative techniques applied equally to all and measured by an archaic rule. If convents perish it will not be for lack of human understanding. They will collapse from the repression of it."

The lack of intellectual freedom and the repression of human emotion seem to head the list of complaints. Typical are the remarks of a former principal of a Catholic high school: "From an intellectual point of view, convents are notoriously stifling. Private judgments and individual opinions are kept in subservient position to the established Rule. One is continually caught in a tragic conflict between vowed commitment to the Rule and the legitimate responsibility to oneself as an individual. To ignore this responsibility is to commit intellectual and moral suicide."

A sociology professor who also left the convent within the past year goes further still: "Traditional convent environment is detrimental to personal and intellectual growth. The spirit of dependency which is fostered and indeed demanded is a denial of that individual freedom which Aquinas so lucidly defended and which the Church today is trying to uphold. Convents will eventually disappear, if for no other reason than that freedom must prevail."

Will convents ultimately perish or can they be reformed before they lose the affectionate place in the hearts of those they once illumined?

A great majority of those who have left religious life are dubious about meaningful or lasting reforms. Some go as far as to say that it is impossible to reform the basic structure of religious life and agree that convents are destined to become obsolete and useless in the context of modern society. Asked to comment on the validity of these conclusions, Sister Francetta agreed that "convent life is no longer relevant to the woman's changing status in society."

The existing crisis is aggravated by the lack of vocations. Ancient religious orders, which a decade ago were processing one hundred or more applications a year, are receiving less than half as many. The young people of today are looking to the Peace Corps, civil and human rights movements, and other such organizations, where they are not called upon to sacrifice their personal and intellectual freedoms and where they can find a greater measure of fulfillment and satisfaction of their apostolic zeal. Today's youth, as witnessed by the restive atmosphere in our universities, is determined to reach personal decisions in the knowledge that they themselves have overruled all other alternatives. To those who prize freedom, their actions seem no less precious for their occasional errors. The authoritarian atmosphere of convent life, they feel, is incompatible with their approach to a democratic way of life. As one young Catholic Peace Corps applicant puts it, "Reverence for God is shown in our respect for Man. We have the responsibility of at least striving for its approximation and we can best do that by freely becoming involved in the total good of all and not in the prescribed and immediate salvation of the few."

Not all the harsh criticism comes from those who have recently left the convent or from those who want no part of it. A young nun educator deplores the existing conditions in equally sharp terms.

"It is clear," she says, "that the individualist who questions, whose intellectual curiosity forces her to seek the answers, the one who is restless to join the army of social revolutionaries, must either leave the convent or place the price tag of silence and acquiescence on her aspirations."

If the number of women who leave the convents daily is increasing, the number of those who remain because they imagine it is too late or too hard to come out is thought to be greater still. Recently I spoke to one such nun who no doubt wanted assurances before taking the final step. "I have been thinking about it for ten years," she said, "and I know that there are others who feel as I do." Similar comments are repeated with frightening frequency by middle-aged women who have spent most of their adult lives in the convent. With most, the problem of deciding whether to stay in or come out goes much deeper than a simple personal decision. These women are genuinely concerned with the role of the Church in ecumenical social thinking and with the Church's traditional role in changing and shaping society. Almost all agree that the post-conciliar Church will continue to be the repository of wisdom and their constant source of enlightenment. But at the same time they seriously question the value of convent life in today's society and its contribution to personal and community growth. The consensus among the critics seems to be that convents, intentionally or not, by their very nature block the flood-gates of progress and create a vacuum which strangles the mind.

There are some who contend that the apostolic mission of the Church can more effectively be accomplished by the zealous and dedicated layman who is not hampered by out-moded traditions and controls and who is anxious and will-ing to attain his rightful place in the Church. It may per-haps be coincidental that the Vatican Council, in response to the needs of modern society, came to recognize the right-ful place of the layman in the Church by elevating him from a passive observer in the wings to an active partici-pant in the center of the stage.

Flowing out of these harsh realities is the conviction that the very existence of the Church depends on its involve-ment in social solidarity in order to fit into the reality of a fast-moving, pluralistic, liberty-loving society. An undeni-able fact is that the news today is being made by the new-style layman, the social reformer, and occasionally by the tough-minded religious who is willing to get involved and, more often than not, without ecclesiastical endowment. It is claimed that the old institutions, unreformed as they stand today, while firmly locked in our sentimental past, lack the force of our social present. These are facts which demand scrutiny by the social conscience of every Catholic. In the light of the Church's neoteric thinking, it is not incon-ceivable to many that convents may become (as did the use of Latin in the Mass) victims of the Church's determination to move ahead with the times.

There are those, on the other hand, who believe that the role of the nun as an educator, social worker, hospital administrator, among her many other traditional functions, is too important to be completely abolished. Out of the present debate on means and ends, methods and practices, bureaucracy and nonconformism, there is emerging an in-surgent breed, with clearly defined features of what appears to be a group of singularly visionary innovators. "The sole purpose," as one sister puts it, "is to seek a universal and contemporary expression of that love which first awakened our desire to serve humanity. It should embrace both the divine and the *human*, thus permitting a more complete fulfillment of the individual."

This revolutionary movement, admittedly not accepted by the majority of the present-day nuns, would seek to eliminate the three vows of poverty, chastity, and obedience and to some extent the traditional and somewhat inflexible rule of communal life. "There is no clear-cut blueprint. It could take many patterns," Sister Francetta told me. "There is no reason why there cannot exist in the Church a group of vowless committed people, with provisions for those who desire or elect to live a celibate life." Personally, Sister Francetta questions "the validity of canonical vows if the sisters are seriously committed to live in and for the contemporary world."

While the concept of a vowless sisterhood appears on the surface to be more revolutionary than any other reform so far suggested, one advocate of the proposed change explained how for centuries wholly dedicated members of non-Catholic religious groups have been conducting missionary, social, and educational programs with the same and sometimes greater effectiveness than Catholic nuns and without the hindrance of religious vows.

In response to the stern demands of conscience, the new breed of sisters is willing to venture forth in faith, in the conviction that the convent as it exists today can serve only as an apprenticeship but not as a final destination. "The love of God is active everywhere," one sister comments. "It is intolerable to think that God intended a person's freedom of response to be limited, even by vows. Love cannot be imprisoned in just one form of expression. It must be free so that others can see their relation to it."

It is possible that the Church may someday accept the

concept of a vowless sisterhood. Mother Eileen, of the Ursuline House of Studies in Washington, D.C., finds no incompatibility in this concept. "There is room in the Church for all." Personally, the vows have a special significance for Mother Eileen. The vow of chastity, in particular, she explains, enables the nun to free herself from the demands and obligations concomitant with marriage. "Because of it we have more availability and disposability—at the service of all."

Sister Melathon, of the Washington Urban Center, also considers that the idea may not be totally alien to the thinking of the post-conciliar Church. She does not feel, however, that her vows prevent a rapport with her environment: "I do not agree with the contention that the vows detract from my living out the rational meaning of what my faith contains."

Some hold, however, that most religious orders, even those which claim to have implemented some measures of reform, cannot bear close examination of these statements. Ecclesiastical discipline is as old as the Catholic Church itself, and the inflexible structures it has created do not permit the total involvement envisioned by the would-be reformers. For these, a more radical change in the entire structure of religious life is imperative. They feel that a new and different kind of religious commitment is coming into being, one that does not require the separation, isolation, and exclusion which the present-day convent life demands. They affirm that the trend, while slow, is inevitably toward the commitment of the total person to the real demands of the common good, seeking to meet not only the spiritual but also the human need, including their own needs as well.

"Not all nuns have the ability or temperament to sublimate their emotional needs," one sister contends, "but most of the ignorance of the Middle Ages in this respect still remains." She claims that until recently the subject of chastity and all its implications has been treated with almost complete silence and a certain amount of fear. Father Albert Plé, O. P., finds no better proof of this than in the constitution of a religious order founded in the seventeenth century by a Dominican, in which article 29 reads: "The nuns must never look at their body except their hands; and even that shall be done as little as possible." "The policy of silence," Father Plé continues, "has shown itself too harmful to be maintained. Pope Pius XII himself condemned it in his speech to the Carmelite Fathers, gathered in Rome to celebrate the twenty-fifth anniversary of their international college."

In her contribution to the book *La Chasteté et problèmes de la religieuse d'aujourd'hui,* Dr. Suzy Rousset warns that a "religious vocation does not create a sexless woman. None of her deep-rooted instincts are removed. The heart still retains its yearning and the same conditions for its development and the leading of a natural life. The nun does not repudiate in herself the bio-psychological foundation in which her capacity for love is rooted. Refusal to believe this and the denial of its existence by imagining herself of an angelic nature is to prepare the way for disaster." Despite these deep-rooted instincts, the nun is capable of sublimating her needs to a higher end. History is a witness to the hundreds of thousands of nuns who through the ages have vowed and faithfully kept the gift of a pure heart to God. "This is possible," Dr. Rousset continues, "when a person's whole behavior is in conformity with the motive laid down by conscience, when the forces wholly subdued to the spirit are made to serve the ends of a genuine ideal, thus sharing in its depth and transcendence. It is then that the expression of an authentically religious motive is integrated into the whole personality and contributes to its unification."

Although there have been some irresponsible and un-

proven accusations against nuns' moral behavior, these have
been in the most part wholly discredited. The striking
example of their lives, amply confirmed by history, indi-
cates that nuns almost in their totality have remained faithful to their vow. This fact alone gives credibility to Dr.
Rousset's statements. Conversely, it is argued that Dr. Rousset's theories on sublimation provide an equally cogent
argument in favor of the dissenters' position against canonical vows. The scope of the "genuine ideal" and the "motive
laid down by conscience" cannot be bound by the thinking
of another age. The role of the woman has evolved through
the centuries and the needs and demands of today are not
those of the early Church. It is claimed that the essential
inequity of the vow of celibacy is that it is exclusive and
that to a degree it betrays, at least in this age, an absence of
Christian charity. Because the age demands that charity be
a living reality and because it requires the total personal involvement of the individual, there is of necessity an ensuing
conflict which prevents the inner, if not the overt, behavior
of a great number of nuns from being "in conformity."
When this happens, within the present convent structure,
there is no place for the nun to go but out.

Those who wish to remain faithful to their religious vocation want an alternative. They are not necessarily dissatisfied with all the aspects of religious life. There are strong
bonds which make community exercises a real and meaningful spiritual experience. There are ties of affection and
common purpose. A vowless religious community, it is con-
tended, would remove the obstacles which prevent a nun
from living her life, as Sister Francetta puts it, "in the sacrament of today." She defends her choice of a religious
vocation. "It came at a time of a different world and it was
relevant to it then. Were I eighteen today I would choose a
different form, but the same commitment. My ideals have
not changed, only my expression of them." These, she ex-

plains, must now meet the needs of the contemporary world
as well as her own needs as an individual.

It is generally agreed, if not publicly at least privately,
that the new theology of social change is slowly but stub-
bornly penetrating convent life. The Most Reverend Francis
Simons, highly respected Bishop of Indore, India, adds a
new concept of morality to it: "The experience of mankind
has to be heeded. Some earlier judgments have been dis-
carded with the spiritual progress of mankind, with the
sharpening of man's judgment. By making the good of mankind the criterion of moral obligation, we bring morality,
which otherwise seems to be hanging in the air, down to
earth, and give it reasonable, practical, and convincing
foundations. God made everything on earth for the sake of
man. He imposed laws only for man's good, and love is the
fulfillment of the law. It is by making herself a slave to the
letter of the formulated laws and not attending to the
underlying spirit that the Church barred for itself the way
to a fuller understanding and a sounder application of her
own basic beliefs."

It is to these issues that the would-be vowless nuns
address themselves. They defend their posture with intellectual cogency believing that their dissension contributes
to the vitality and true purpose of the Church. They seek to
be a part of the new climate of freedom, including freedom
from uniformity, which they claim grows out of habit and is
often devoid of the enormous reality of faith. They pose an
unprecedented challenge to the Church's traditional posture
that the nun is "in the world but not of it." In short, they
claim the legitimacy and the right to be human with all the
demands and obligations which this right implies, for themselves in particular and for mankind in general.

Latin America: The Celibacy Gap

Paul Hagan

*FATHER PAUL HAGAN, forty-five, is a native of Philadel-
phia (New York). He received his early education in public
schools, and in 1940 became a candidate for the priesthood
at Wadhams Hall Seminary, Ogdensburg (New York). In
1944 he entered the major seminary of St. Bernard's, Roch-
ester (New York), and was ordained in 1947. From 1947 to
1957 he served as assistant pastor in two New York state
parishes, then was appointed pastor of St. John's parish,
Morristown (New York), where he served for five years.
Since 1962 Father Hagan has been in Latin America. During his first year of missionary service he studied in the
Maryknoll language school in Bolivia and worked with
Maryknoll missionary priests in both Bolivia and Peru.
Since 1963 he has been pastor of St. Martin de Porres
parish in Mollendo, Peru. Together with several other
priests, seminarians, and university students, Father Hagan
has been collecting sociological data in the Andes for use in
a study sponsored by the local bishop for the purpose of
developing better understanding of the culture and basic
aspirations of the people he is committed to serve.*

North Americans used to look rather condescendingly on their South American neighbors. They saw the majority of them as easygoing, siesta-loving types, poor, but satisfied and happy. Governments were thought of as passing clumsily from the hands of one inept group to another. The United States government did what it could for these simple people, knowing that it would not really do much good until they grew up.

Now this view is changing. The big stick used to correct naughty children was finally put away by Kennedy. Even though there have been strong divergencies from his enlightened policies, especially in the Dominican fiasco, a more realistic view has emerged. Many Peace Corps volunteers have seen the realities of Latin American life. These people will affect general attitudes and government policy.

I hope the North American view of the Latin American Church is changing too. It is not a weak brother that can be saved by a massive influx of North American personnel, or that magic cure-all, "money and know-how." The Church in South America is not run by poorly educated, concubinate clergy walking around in dirty cassocks, nor is it concerned exclusively with educating the rich and maintaining the *status quo*. It is a Church of change, of contradictions, of clashing opinions. There is violence and passivity. There are priests who are money grabbers and others who are living in exemplary poverty with their people. Nuns who have chosen poverty live in elegance alongside fellow Christians crushed by destitution. Other nuns in priestless areas are running parishes like deaconesses. Once a month the priest visits the area for Mass and the other days the sisters distribute Communion, preach, teach, baptize, and generally shepherd the flock. There are bishops who literally live in castles, and others who live in slums. One bishop came back from the council with silver buckles for the canons of the cathedral and others with a renewed view of the Church. There are dioceses where all foreign clergy are welcome regardless of their pastoral training. There are other dioceses where only those are welcome who will work in teams with native and foreign priests in a developed pastoral plan. Chile has a pastoral plan for the entire nation based on the scientific studies of the famous Bellarmine Institute in Santiago. The Church is self-critical and complacent, open and closed, fresh and stagnant, liberal and reactionary, rich and poor, pretridentine and avant-garde. No label fits.

It is against this background that you must read what I write. Some may disagree with what I say, but I can only report what I see and feel based on my life here and many discussions with our poor, a few socially minded rich, and many committed South American and foreign clergy.

The South American is very much socially and family oriented. There are rare occasions when I am alone. If a parishioner comes to the house and finds me in this "sad" state he will exclaim, "You're alone!" and sit and wait, occasionally at considerable inconvenience, until someone else comes. I thought I had a reputation for suicidal tendencies until I found other gringos have the same experience. North Americans value being alone at times, but here in Peru it is dreaded.

It is hard for a North American to imagine what a tragedy it is to be without a family here. When we use the word orphan we think of children. Here a man of seventy may refer to himself as an orphan. If a man is sick or in hard straits his story begins, "Father, I'm an orphan. No family. My parents, godparents, my brothers and cousins are all dead." Then he will tell me about his sickness or financial troubles, but the worst tragedy is being an orphan.

In one town I was visiting, a drunk came by and talked for a while. When he left I asked one of the other men, "Is he an alcoholic, or just celebrating?" "Sure, he's an alcoholic," he said, "he has no family." I've found out that in this town of fifteen hundred people there are eight alcoholics. All except one live alone.

The Latin American is pre-eminently a family man. It is taken for granted that he will marry. The sexual urge in the male is considered so irresistible that the education of youth must be separate. Government and private schools are seldom coeducational. Dating must be extremely well chaperoned. If boys or girls should happen not to marry they never live alone. They live with their parents or married brothers and sisters. Almost all the people in old folks' homes are orphans. Grandparents always live with their children. The privacy that the old and single claim to want in North America is not desired here. Three generations live in almost every house. Not only are aunts and uncles considered part of the family, but the *compadres* too—those who were witnesses at weddings or were godparents. *Compadres* are included in the family circle for feast days and celebrations. In public and private, relatives and *compadres* are referred to by their title. As soon as a best friend becomes godfather of a child, his first name ceases to exist. He is addressed simply as *compadre* and referred to as my *compadre* Michael. An uncle or a cousin might be called Uncle Joe or Cousin Joe, but never just Joe.

The South American has much to teach us about living and loving. There exists what one wise South American priest describes as an affective atmosphere or *ambiente*. The

South American loves children, womanhood, and his friends in a warm, demonstrative way that North Americans find embarrassing. South American men do not shake hands every time they meet; they embrace friends and occasionally kiss them. I was in a restaurant last summer with another priest and three North American seminarians. A stranger singled out one of the seminarians and started praising him. "I love Americans," he said, "and here is a real American. Look how beautiful he is: tall, fair, blond, strong. Here is a typical American. Isn't he beautiful?" And the four ugly ducklings with him stuttered out: "Oh, he's beautiful, all right."

But the highly developed affective sensibilities of the Latin American focus primarily on womanhood. North American girls are at first very flattered by the attention shown them until they find out that this attention is shown to all girls.

The style of living here is perhaps best described as *carinoso,* meaning affectionate, tender, kind. It is indicative of the difference between North and South Americans that this very important word cannot be accurately translated into English. There is no one word in the English language that has the same connotation. This is true also of many words to which *ito* and *ita* are attached. We easily translate *Padre* as Father, but we can't translate *Padrecito.* It adds the concepts of friendship, love, familiarity, and tenderness. Last year a young Peruvian seminarian accompanied me to a school run by nuns. When the sister answered the door, I addressed her as *Madre.* Afterward the seminarian told me that *Madre* is too cold and formal. I should have said, *"Madrecita."*

The Church could hardly ignore this atmosphere. What was its response?

The Church could have taught the beauty of passions. It could have urged the growth, development, and expression of the tenderness, the warmth, the affective powers of these peoples. It could have pointed to avenues of creative expression. It could have shown the great possibilities for contributions to the world by these naturally expressive and tender people.

Unfortunately it did not. The teaching of the Church was negative and repressive. Man was corrupted by original sin. He was basically bad. His passions proved this. Passions were not to be developed, built upon, expressed, or even channeled. They were to be crushed. The joyous feast of Christmas, the rising expectations of the Resurrection, the energizing presence of the Holy Spirit have no place in popular piety even today. These happy people have been fed a religion of tears and masochistic penance. Penance is gauged not by the charity it leads to, but by the pain it causes. Good Friday is *the* feast with no relation to the Ressurrection or to the rest of the Church year. This is truly a religion of the "death of God" which antedates Bonhoeffer by centuries.

Statues are tear-stained and bloody. Crucifixes have a pitifully whipped, torn, mangled victim spiked to the cross. They are decorated with the tools of torture. A glorious, jeweled crucifix is almost unknown. Hymns sound like funeral dirges. The words shine forth of a downtrodden, worthless people. In one popular hymn, *Oh Buen Jesús,* the congregation sings in singular, "Jesus sees only my nothingness, my sinfulness. I confess shamefully my unworthiness." In another old favorite, *De Rodillas,* we sing to the Lord "from our knees, with our forehead in the dust." Hard on the diaphragm, but supposedly good for the soul. All this one-sided, depressing piety has been foisted on a bubbling, expansive, passionate, fun-loving people. The argument seems to be: the passions are bad, but these are a passionate people. Therefore, they are bad.

Above all, the sexual drive is seen as bad and uncontrol-

lable, especially in men. As a result children are separated
early. The girls are taught in separate and unequal schools.
A boy and girl are never to be left alone.

The sexual morality taught these students is fantastic.
Last year a priest who specializes in retreats for high school
students preached that it was a mortal sin to have a boy
friend. A Catholic girls' school, where the nuns refer to
Matrimony as the "dirty" Sacrament, has the marriage section of the religion texts taped shut. Any girl breaking the
seal faces immediate expulsion. In some instances retreat
masters still tell students that it is a mortal sin to look at
their own bodies.

The Church here has made the same misleading interpretation of Saint Thomas on marriage that much of the teaching Church made in the rest of the world. The results have
been at least as disastrous. Saint Thomas' distinction of
primary and secondary ends of marriage has been taught as
primary in importance and secondary in importance in spite
of his clear explanation to the contrary. To a loving people
with highly developed sensitivities centering primarily on
womanhood, marriage is said to exist for children. Divorce
is wrong, not because of the nature of love, but because of
the welfare of children.

This popular preaching obviously springs from the seminaries. A Peruvian priest told me that I could not imagine
how bad his training was. He was actually told that if a
woman were to sit beside him on a trolley he should repeat
to himself, "It's a sack of potatoes, it's a sack of potatoes."
Any casual observer knows that either this advice doesn't
work, or it has not been followed. Unfortunately this teaching continues in some instances. In some seminaries students still have to dress and undress in bed! A newly ordained priest recently referred to celibacy, in contrast to
love, as "the priestly life." But in practice he sees "the

priestly life" as quite dispensable. He tells me he will marry as soon as the Church changes the law.

The teaching of the Church has clashed sharply with the South American temperament. The result has not been a change in approach by the Church, but rather an intensification of a teaching of the evil of man and his world, the glory of heaven, and the pain of hell.

The faithful have given nodding assent to what has been taught. They fully agree that man and the world are bad. Therefore, the doctrine of the Church concerning sexual morality may be very true, but it is impossible to live by. No man can remain pure between seven and seventy. Sexual expression is as necessary as food and drink. Prostitution is legalized. It is unjust, but to many minds necessary for the protection of good girls.

The people see a conflict between what is taught as true and what they experience as true. To a certain extent they are right. How long can a starving people be told that the world and its goods are evil? Science is emerging. Fatalism is dying. These people want a theology that takes the world seriously. They have never given internal assent to a theology that relegated love to a secondary place in marriage.

There has been a difference between reality and what was taught. It would seem that this has had much to do with the problem of communication here. It is very common to give the answer the questioner wants to hear rather than the truthful answer. If I invite people to a meeting they will all tell me they will come—whether they intend to or not. They know this is the answer I want to hear. Occasionally I can recognize the "yes" that means "no," but not always. It leads to doubt of anyone's word—a real breakdown in communication, trust, and confidence.

It is very difficult for a celibate priest in this milieu. Often he is in an isolated area, two or three days by bus, horse, or mule from the culture of a city. Frequently 95 percent of his parishioners are Indians whose language he does not know. He has received no instruction in the people's culture and frequently treats them paternalistically. Neither his education nor his cultural background has prepared him to accept them as equals worthy of friendship. He is isolated from family and friends. He is frequently the only educated man in town. His highest cultural contact would be a few radio stations. Plays, movies, TV, and good restaurants are non-existent. We know of one rural area of forty thousand people in small scattered villages with only two priests. It is a discouraging situation and very common.

Isolation and huge numbers of people would be debilitating for a celibate clergy in any society. Here, however, other factors increase the problem.

The priest knows, for example, of other priests who are living a married life and continuing their ministry. Recently one rural area had thirteen priests, eleven of whom were married. It would seem that the parishioners in the rural areas accept a married pastor even more readily than parishioners in the United States accept a pastor who drinks heavily. A friend recently told me about a priest for whom he had great respect because of his brilliance and charity. He sincerely thought this man was the greatest priest he had ever known. The fact that this priest had twelve children did not change his judgment. For years I have heard a local priest criticized for the high prices he charges even the poor for his services, for his meanness to children and general cantankerous disposition. He was never criticized for lack of purity, yet all this time he was living openly with his wife and children. Several factors enter into this response by the faithful.

First of all, most people do not believe any man is faithful to celibacy. Virginity for a man is considered absolutely impossible. All parish priests are suspected of having at least an occasional affair. Rumors fly about priests and bishops who would be completely above suspicion in most other societies. Coupled to a general disbelief in the possibility of celibacy is a sort of cavalier attitude even toward laws considered reasonable. Laws are not "hard and fast," applying to all equally. They are flexible. They bend to the circumstances, the person, and the amount of influence he has.

It must also be remembered that much of the marriage custom predates Trent and the necessity to be married according to the form. Quite generally people are considered married in a common-law union. Many couples live in a common-law marriage before having a civil or religious ceremony. In the minds of the people the union of the priest and his "wife" would be a real marriage, not concubinage.

What is to be done in this situation? A great deal is being done that fills one with hope. Imaginative things are happening. The prophets and men of vision are not isolated voices among the lower clergy fearing censure. Brilliant, imaginative bishops are crying out and being heard. An incarnational theology that identifies injustice fearlessly is being preached. The crushing poverty and hunger of the masses is being faced. In many areas the Church is courageously on the side of the poor. The Church has radio, TV, schools, credit unions, and cooperatives of all types. Peasants are being trained and organized. According to Sidney Lens in a recent article about Christian socialism, bishops, priests, and laymen in all nineteen republics are to be found on the left of the Communists. ("Latin Left." *Commonweal,* Oct. 14, 1966, vol. 85, No. 2.) In Chile, for example, Catholic Action is in trouble because its best men are now in Frei's government. Priests are busy training new leaders. The Brazilian government has exiled priests because of their social teaching. Centers of socio-religious studies, such as the Bellarmine Institute in Chile, are operating in Buenos Aires and Montevideo as well. The Dominicans in Bolivia are doing a national grass-roots study that will provide their bishops with social, anthropological, and religious data. A great effort is being made to gather the facts for a relevant preaching of the gospel. This is vitally important. In most places the Church is still greatly respected and influential. By addressing itself to real problems it can do much to restore communication, to strengthen the relationship between what is said and what is actually believed in all society. It is bound to have an invigorating effect on the priests too. They will have the confidence of men working on serious problems in an intelligent way.

In some dioceses priests are not sent out to work alone, but work in teams, praying and living together. Not only are the Little Brothers and Little Sisters of Jesus in several areas, but Argentina has its own priest-worker experiment. Chile, Brazil, and Peru have asked for the restoration of the diaconate. It is interesting that in Peru no celibates will be ordained deacons. Candidates must have been married for at least ten years. Seminaries are being updated in many places. The Archdiocese of Arequipa, Peru, is experimenting with three different types of seminaries next year. One group will live at the seminary and take classes there as usual. Another group will live at the seminary, but take their classes at the coeducational Catholic University. The third group will live in a rented house and attend the University.

These changes are excellent, but they will not fill the need of a sharp increase in a well-trained native clergy. Even with the projected increase in the number of foreign clergy, the ratio of priests to parishioners is getting worse. Allan Holmberg of Cornell University pointed out that the population of Peru, for example, will double between 1964 and 1974 (Allan Holmberg: West Point Conference on Latin American Problems, 1964).

At the end of the council Pope Paul suggested a Holy Year. Dom Helder Camara was enthusiastic. Make it a real year of healing and forgiveness, he suggested. Remove all censures, interdicts, and suspensions. Should this not include the clergy who are married and continuing their ministry? Should the bishop not bless their marriages? This would restore them to a proper sacramental life, remove debilitating shame, and increase the confidence of their flock. Would it not be much better for a bishop to do this than to ignore the situation? And the married clergy who are not practicing their ministry, could they not be married by their bishop and encouraged to return to their priestly functions? It would seem that the needs of the Church and the mercy of Christ cry out for these healing acts.

It is certainly a fact that many men dedicated to the Church have not entered the seminary, or have left it, because of celibacy. Many are in Catholic Action. Could they not be ordained to the priesthood? It would include men from a variety of professions and backgrounds, broadening the scope of the worker-priest experiments and enhancing the priesthood.

Certainly young men training for the secular priesthood should be free to marry. This is not just a ploy to increase numbers. More native priests are urgently needed and the Church has the duty to find them. But the results would be more far-reaching. Currently the people do not believe the priest is faithful to celibacy. Its meaning will only be clear to them when they see that it is embraced freely by a man who could marry at any time. Only under these conditions could the people begin to see and understand the beauty of celibacy. Secondly, the priest's relationship with women is very artificial. Much suspicion surrounds any contact he has with them. This could be greatly improved if priests were either married or voluntarily celibate.

A married diaconate is, of course, a step in the right direction, but it does not help the present generation of seminarians, or the many married clergy. These men must be offered a full, respectable place in the Church. The day may not be far off. Some feel the married diaconate is a diplomatic ploy toward that goal. After the Peruvian national hierarchy petitioned for the married diaconate, one of the bishops was asked when they were going to recognize their married priests. "Not now," he said a little nervously, "later, later." Not all bishops have been so indirect. Following a meeting in Buenos Aires of eighty priests, two bishops, and several theologians to discuss voluntary celibacy, Bishop Peter Koop of Brazil wrote this urgent warning for the Vatican Council: "We have to make a choice right away: either to multiply the number of priests both celibate and married, or look forward to the collapse of the Church in South America."

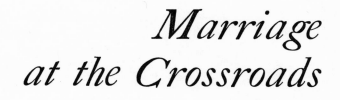

Marriage
at the Crossroads

Charles Long

CHARLES W. LONG was born February 23, 1934, in Louisville, Kentucky. He attended a Catholic grade school in Jeffersonville, Indiana, and St. Xavier High School, Louisville. He spent six years at St. Meinrad Seminary, St. Meinrad, Indiana, and four years at the Theological College of the Catholic University of America. On May 3, 1960, he was ordained a Roman Catholic priest. From 1960 to 1964 Father Long worked as assistant pastor, Holy Family Church, New Albany, Indiana. He was then transferred to St. Mary-Michael parish, Madison, Indiana, where he remained until 1966. On February 5, 1966, he married the former Ruth E. Biere. Mr. and Mrs. Long now reside in Alexandria, Virginia.

The day my bishop clasped my hands and asked for a pledge of obedience—a pledge including obedience to my vow of lifelong celibacy—the day of my ordination, I gave that pledge willingly. And the day—seven years later—that I held my bride's hand, I pledged my love to her just as willingly. How a man can in good faith make these apparently contradictory pledges is a question I hope to answer in this essay; and in answering it, I hope to speak for the many married priests who are, like me, wrongfully labeled "ex-priests."

Aside from having the misfortune of being a favorite of Sister Superior in my parochial grade school, of being, according to sister, "a boy that surely has a vocation," I had no special "sign" of a vocation, although I had always concurred with my parents' belief that "Father" was a necessary part of every Catholic's life. I went to high school with the idea of being a good athlete and a "regular guy"; but I thought more about becoming a priest. More and more the priesthood seemed to me the ideal way of serving God and man; and a retreat to the Trappist Abbey of Gethsemani—where, in an atmosphere of serenity and spartan living, the life of prayer seems almost a life of adventure—convinced me that the priesthood was truly my vocation.

Because I was relatively sure of my vocation, my early days in the seminary were pleasant; there were no psychic traumas, no painful battles of conscience. As far as the

179

problem of celibacy was concerned, it troubled me little until college, when the question of whether celibacy is really necessary—whether it is really a good—often came up. During those days, not a few seminarians were secretly dating girls from the nearby town. I was somewhat shocked by this, but not nearly so shocked as I was by the almost neurotic reaction of the rector and spiritual director when they discovered that seminarians were dating these girls. In anger, both of these men delivered ultimatums amounting to: "Quit dating or get out of the seminary." The tone of their remarks caused me to remember the remarks made about a parish assistant who, when I was in grade school, had married a woman of our parish. The man was kind and dedicated, a competent, hard-working priest, indeed, by virtually everyone's standards, an excellent priest. But when he married, he was through, washed up. There were those who condemned him, those who spoke of him condescendingly—"Well, you can't expect all of them to make it; even Christ lost one of His apostles"—and those who piously refused to pass judgment. But there were a few who wondered: Why celibacy? Why should this fine priest not be able to perform his ministry? And that question remained an ember in my unconscious, I suppose, for it flared up during those college days in the seminary.

Although they taught us in theology that there is a great difference between ecclesiastical and divine law, when it came to celibacy in particular and chastity in general, they made the gap appear awfully narrow. And during my college days I and, I venture to say, most of my fellow seminarians, were confused by the lack of consistency on the Church's part concerning celibacy and unconvinced that celibacy equaled sanctity. Although I soon became a "priest forever," as I look back, I can see that during my seminary days in college I had clearly decided what most young priests, I think, decide: that celibacy is not *per se* a good, but rather a necessary burden, a *conditio sine qua non* for entering the priesthood. To be sure, celibacy has the practical advantage of guaranteeing that the priest will not have the economic and psychological responsibilities of a family, but that, for *every* priest, is certainly not an advantage; in fact, as I shall show later, it can definitely harm the vocations of many priests.

The days of my early ministry were pleasant enough. I was not suffering from intense passion or searching for a reason to leave the priesthood. I grew restless, not because of celibacy, but because I was becoming convinced that the service I could render men was being hampered rather than aided by much of what was prescribed as "priestly activity." "Feeding the hungry, clothing the naked, and healing the sick," became a farce in a parish devoted to organizing Bingo games and conducting novenas. The irrelevance of speculative theology and meaningless devotions made me yearn to work at my true vocation—encountering Christ in others. And it was at this stage in my career that I met my wife, who understood my needs because her needs were the same. At first we fought our love for each other; we sought advice from confessors, prayed, tried to think it out. We knew that, should we marry, it would appear that we were choosing each other rather than God. But we knew that really we were not rejecting God, but accepting Him all the more; we knew that our marriage and my vocation were *the* vocation that God willed us.

To those who will say: "You're rationalizing," we can only answer that we know we are violating existing Church law, but that is a law that can and should be changed. Most important, we are not violating our own consciences. There was no undue pressure for us to marry—no pregnancy, no feeling that it was impossible to remain in that situation. The driving force was, I repeat, simply love for each other and the sense that it was our vocation to serve others together. If our needs had been merely sexual, we would have been better off to have had an affair, without making any commitment to each other. If we had merely wanted an escape, we were paying a terrific price for an escape that could have been had at discount.

For my wife our marriage has meant leaving home without parental blessing, being told by the Church that she is a great sinner, having to enter into a life where struggle is the daily fare and security ever doubtful. For me it has meant resigning the practice of a ministry I loved, being looked upon as a reject and "ex" this or that, and accepting human responsibilities that far outweigh those I had known in the five years prior to our marriage.

But we are happily married, expecting a child, and working with an ecumenical group on a project that enables us to offer food and shelter to people coming into our area seeking jobs—people who need spiritual as well as material help. We also continue to receive the Sacraments. How can we receive the Sacraments, how can we continue to function as Catholics? The simplest answer is that we just do. Experience after experience of married priests seeking satisfactory juridical decisions that would enable them to function as priests and yet be married has proven that such decisions, at the moment, are impossible. Therefore, my wife and I employ a situational ethics approach whereby we have made a judgment: that Canon Law does not provide a remedy that is sensible in view of the present situation of the Church, the world, and ourselves. Most of the priests we know don't hesitate to give us the Sacraments. There is much greater freedom in such matters than most people will admit.

Thousands of potentially fine priests have left or will leave the priesthood because of the Church's intransigent attitude toward celibacy, and the question is, *why?* These thousands are forced to leave because something in religious life itself renders them sterile and deprives them of an opportunity for a love hardly understood in rectories and convents because it combines the divine and human. Maybe it is poetic to say that one who unites himself or herself in love to the world and to a mate can have a deeper insight into the Incarnate love, the perfect combination of human and divine, but nevertheless I am willing to say just that. And I am willing to suggest that until the Church changes its rule on celibacy the great declines that have been taking place in religious vocations of all kinds will continue.

Like Father Anthony Girandola, the married priest in St. Petersburg, Florida, who has opened a refuge for other priests in his situation, I feel that it is my duty not simply to "fade away" into oblivion (as so many married priests before me have done), but to continue to assert my belief that I have a right to both marriage and the priesthood, that it is not priests like Father Girandola and myself who are wrong, but the Church law which is wrong. As the successful civil rights workers in America have done, we must protest unjust laws by openly testifying in our lives to their injustice. I know of priests who could help my wife and me obtain Church validation of our marriage, but at what price? First, I would have to agree never to exercise my priestly powers again. Second, I would have to obey a law requiring me never to reveal my previous state of life in the parish where I would receive the Sacraments. But this would only be a perpetuation of hypocrisy and a denial of one of my fundamental rights. It is my conviction that priests like myself and Father Girandola must (as Father DuBay has, for other causes) act publicly to pressure the Church, through the bishops, to re-examine its stand on celibacy. Not long ago contraception was thought to be a closed issue, but public pressure opened it; and the same thing can happen to the "closed issue" of celibacy.

Now I realize that should celibacy be abolished for the

active ministry, a substantial revamping of the clerical life as we know it would be necessary. Therefore, I would like to present some suggestions for what the priestly ministry might become in the future. To meet the needs of city and suburban dwellers, the priest would get away from the *sanctum sanctorum* of the rectory and live among the people.

More important, he would earn his living as other people do, not from service in the Church, but out in the world. (This would, of course, require a thorough revamping of the educational process leading to ordination. The traditional seminary curriculum would be a far from adequate preparation for coping with the economic realities of an independent life in the secular milieu.) Such a life, combined with his sacramental power conferred at ordination and with his theological training, would make the priest a true liturgical leader of his Church's people.

His life, of course, would not be easy: The priest would have to support his family; he would have to prove himself worthy of a job or of success on his own merits, not on the strength of his Roman collar; he would soon see that the image of God that priests have so long been preaching is not a big part of the layman's life; and he would soon realize that if he wants to lead his community—if he wants to hold his spiritual flock together—he can never settle (as priests in the present system regularly settle) for mediocrity, but must always strive for excellence.

All of this may seem like the twilight zone, and in a sense it is. The more pressing problem is how those of us who are married and ordained can serve the Church today. We could serve if the Church permitted us to assist those priests in our areas in offering the Eucharist and in administering other Sacraments. We could become mediators between the functioning clergy and the laity, sharing with the clergy and with laymen our unique experiences as family men. Would such a situation work? Who can really know unless it is tried?

Finally, I would like to urge those who are in the same situation as my wife and I not to despair, although there are many causes for despair. Unbelievable as it may sound, I know of a priest in a large city who has an obsession for tracking down "ex-priests" and using every pressure to make them and their wives either leave their "lives of sin" or, at least, move out of town. That such a man can operate with the tacit approval of the Church's authorities is beyond belief for a Christian.

Even greater, however, than "clear and present dangers" such as the above, is the ever-present danger of despair from guilt, the result of which may well be a total discarding of any concern for the Church in any area. To combat this despair, I think the only hope is to retain our commitment to Christ and the Church in the Eucharist. If we continue to believe that this sacrament is a visible sign of our union with Christ and one another, we have the opportunity to keep our membership in the internal and external form of the Church.

I encourage priests and their wives to receive the Eucharist because of my belief that the Incarnate Christ presents Himself to all men. He does not accept or reject them. They have to make this decision—this decision we call faith. In the offering of the Eucharist to the people of God by Christ's representatives, the same state remains. All those who have faith in the Real Presence have to decide whether they are worthy or not to receive His Body and Blood. This decision cannot be made by a priest at the Communion table or by the Holy Father himself. Even though this reception is a public act of the total community, I cannot see where the community has a right to decide who will and who will not receive, providing the recipients have faith. To hold otherwise is to place Christ in a position in which He did not place Himself. It is in the Eucharist now, as before, that I feel my wife and I publicly profess our love of Christ, of each other, and of all mankind. This source of unity cannot be overlooked by any of us who are supposedly "cut off."

That anything will come of all of this will depend on the validity of my hypothesis that there are many couples like us who wish to continue serving the Church, the husband at the altar breaking bread with the community just as he does with his family. If there are many, the outlook can be bright. If few, we will have to lean more heavily on the charity and understanding of those bishops who really know what is going on around them.

Whatever the case, there are many at the same crossroads that we passed recently, and there will be many more. If the Church wishes, it can erect signs at the intersection which will lead to the road of abundant new life for those at the crossroads as well as for the Church. If the Church does not erect signs, the travelers will continue on without the Church's help and—though enduring unnecessary confusion and suffering—will survive.

Fallen Angels

Victor Venete

For personal reasons the author of this essay has chosen a pseudonym. He was educated for the priesthood and ordained in Europe where, from 1939 to 1949, he served as assistant pastor and pastor. In 1949 he came to the United States, functioning as a parish priest for eighteen months in the New York Archdiocese. He married in 1952, and for a short time served in the ministry of the Episcopal Church. For the past fifteen years he has been in the employ of a large Eastern university.

I am not bitter against the Church; I never was. I do not detract from her divine or human virtues. But I have been disenchanted with the law of ecclesiastical celibacy ever since I opened my eyes to the realities of life. I believe I am justified in manifesting my disapproval.

I grew up under the jealous custody of one of my elder sisters and the strict discipline of a priest who was my private Latin tutor. She was a sincere Victorian; he was a phony Puritan. I was the innocent liaison between him and his girl friend. I used to carry presents and messages. I understood their sentimental relationship when once I surprised them tenderly holding hands in the sacristy of a church. It was my first shock before I went to the seminary.

As a seminarian I had a good friend, from another diocese, who was ordained a priest about the same time as I. We kept ourselves in correspondence as priests, and his letters were full of fire for the apostolate. I loved him and he was an inspiration to me. Suddenly his letters stopped, despite persistent prodding. Later I learned that he had left the priesthood to be married. This was my first shock as a priest. But his was the luminous flight of a young eagle, shot down into darkness and disrepute because he had fallen openly in love. He then lived as a fugitive, and I prayed for him. In the first years of my ministry, a woman from another town came to make her confession to me and

189

told me that for eighteen years she had been as a wife to the priest for whom she kept house, and that she could not continue being "the private prostitute of a priest in good standing." This was my first freeze in the ministry. Though I felt sorry for her, I could not lift my hand to give absolution to this poor victim of the sneaky old fox who periodically slaughtered his prey in the dark and comfortable privacy of his lair, licked his lips clean when he came into the open, and lived as a respected liar, enjoying "two cakes." A beautiful girl used to come and cry at my confessional because a priest was regularly taking her out in his car for erotic motives, and she could not get away from his grip. I blamed but I also pitied him. These are but a few examples of my initial shock and disenchantment. I disapproved of the conduct of the miserable priests, but I disapproved more of the law of the Church. As for myself, I tried to be a good priest while I was one. I respected the human property of legal owners, the marital rights of husbands, and the integrity of single girls. Not that occasions did not offer themselves to me or that I did not have spontaneous offers. But I loved and feared God, honored the law of the Church, prized the reputation of my ministry, repressed desires, and suffered agonies. But in the end I failed when I fell in love. I fell in love and I fled away from love, but love caught up with me. I actually asked my bishop to relieve me as assistant in the main church of my own town and to send me to a village lost on top of a lonely mountain where no priest wished to go or wanted to stay. Even there love reached me. Nature scored its victory and the shell of my innocence was shattered forever. I was offered an honorable transfer—not because of any resulting scandal—but I preferred to transfer myself far, far away: thousands of miles away, to the United States. It did not help. I tried to mend my heart, but the wound did not heal; I tried to chastise my flesh, but the exuberance of nature won the struggle over the resistance of the spirit; I tried to renew my life, but I found out that it is not good for man to be alone.

I consider myself a representative of both European and American clergy: I was born and raised in Europe, and I have been in this country for years. Both here and there I experienced the problems of celibacy and witnessed the frank but cautious opinions of priests; I appraised the sincere and open feelings of deeply religious, honest, and intelligent laymen. I also heard in confession of the painful struggles and of the dismaying failures of good priests in connection with the practice of chastity. Many compromised by honoring celibacy and offending chastity. Perhaps they were the smart ones, and I was a fool. I do not intend to justify my behavior *post factum*, but to expound my convictions *de facto*. I believe the ecclesiastical law on celibacy to be stretched too much and too far to make it rest solely on scriptural foundations and spiritual motives; I believe it to be neither practical nor useful, much extolled and little practiced. Like some other laws of the Church, it seems founded more on convenience than on conviction. It is more for angels and less for men. Its punishments against violators are too severe, inhumane, unjust, and absurd. Its remedies for penitents are cruel and unrealistic. A priest can no longer be a priest if he gets married; the ecclesiastical law supersedes the divine gift of vocation and ordination. Marriage makes him an excommunicated apostate, thus rendering Orders and Matrimony, two great Sacraments, incompatible. While deprived of his privileges of "*Sacerdos in aeternum*," and excluded from the Sacraments, the obligation of enduring celibacy and chastity is still imposed on the wild angel. Thus he cannot be a priest and he cannot be a layman. He is damned to a suspended limbo with no hope of redemption. He is even eligible for hell, with his wife as his custodian devil, unless he should leave the devil to become an angel again! The Church has no heart for a poor wife. The fallen angel is always encouraged to embrace the ideal solution: "abandon her." A married priest is not necessarily a corrupt being or a deserter at heart. He may be an honest man to whom marriage seems, as it is, a more honorable and moral choice than a hypocritical life of compromise between appearance and violation. This latter adaptation may involve somebody's wife. The consequences may be disastrous for both priest and woman. On the other hand, if a priest wants to respect the property of another man or the honor and future of a single girl, he is bound to become a solitary sinner.

In either case, a man-priest is responding to an urge which is stronger than himself—because it is life itself—but in an illicit way. How many victims have we not heard in confession? And confession itself is a weapon of double edge for both priest and woman. In its intimacy married women or single girls get emotionally attached to the priest-confessor, for the spiritual and paternal interest the priest shows to them is often turned into sentimental affection. This is not usually degeneration but a natural process of the human heart. For the priest who lacks the fulfillment of natural and tender affection, it is not easy to resist the penitent who turns gratitude into affection toward a kind but lonesome priestly heart. The Church wants the priest to keep his affection above human level and his heart free from earthly bondage. This is easier said than done. The Church, in fact, often takes a priest when he is a boy of twelve. She keeps him in seclusion or under close vigilance for twelve more years, indoctrinates him with the notion that celibacy is a far superior state of life (something he does not understand yet), and solicits from him a promise of chastity as a condition to becoming a priest. Then she launches him into contact with a world he does not know. He is generally honest and sincere but often naive and inexperienced, and his heart vibrates disturbingly at the first experiences with feminine affection bestowed upon him. I do not know whether there are priest-angels who pass the test without contamination. Perhaps there are, perhaps I know or think I know some who balance themselves well enough. But, after all, the virtue of chastity, as distinct from celibacy, is not self-evident and self-revealing. I know of hypocrites who try to save the appearances but come to a dishonorable compromise; and I know of girls who become enmeshed with priests. A priest, whom I knew very well, once said to his young and beautiful girl friend, "I will kill you if you get married!"

Getting a sign of love from a priest is often esteemed a coveted privilege, and the possession of a place of preference in his heart is a source of rivalry for many women. Dissatisfied wives, exuberant girls, pious penitents know that his heart is free from the pledge to a wife, so that the priest's love is their best desire. Naturally, and more often than not, the attachment does not stop at the soul and heart. *"Post visum risum, post risum tactum, post tactum factum."* (From sight to smile, from smile to touch, from touch to act.) The steps are gradual but fatal. The choice is a lacerating dilemma for the priest: either to keep himself in the ministry and ruin a girl physically and socially, or to leave the priesthood and marry the girl he is in love with, if she is free. If she is not, then he may become a sacrilegious fornicator—and make of her a sacrilegious adulteress. Times have changed and so may the discipline of the Church, especially now that celibacy has become a gem of no real value in the modern world, and scandals and defections are multiplying. Are we more wicked now than before? No, we are more realistic, more frank, and more honest. The voice of protest has not been only that of fallen angels or of ordinary priests, but also of intellectuals, of theologians, of prelates. I can never forget the words of a priest, a friend since boyhood who is now a vicar general. His preaching on morality was uncompromising. He was a sincere, stern practitioner of virtues, as far as I know. Yet, in our private conversation he said to me once: "My ears have heard too many terrible things in the confession of priests in regard to violations of chastity. I wish that our generation will not pass away before a courageous and realistic pope abolishes celibacy as a condition for the priesthood. It would be a blessing for the Church." Well, unfortunately the present Pope took the opposite stand, confirming the unrealistic position of the Church.

Is the Church being selfish? It seems so, because she considers the celibate priest more transferable, more subservient, less expensive. But this is only a veneer. In fact many priests believe their mission. Are they really free from the cares of a family? In Europe a priest often lives with parents. Often he has brothers and sisters, nephews and nieces who expect him to take care of them precisely because he is not married. On the other hand, some are without relatives. They curse life for lack of assistance, live in squalor, go dirty, die alone; or they have a housekeeper. Often she is, in reality, a practical and unlawful wife instead of a registered and lawful one! They beget illegitimate children for whom they have to care in one way or the other; they leave modest to considerable fortunes to relatives or "housekeepers." They are avaricious, selfish, sour, unkind, arid, despondent, drunkards, playboys—and these unfortunately are not rare exceptions. They do not serve God with a joyful heart, but with forbearance and disgust; they do not love people but consider them a nuisance—if they do not hate them. They are irritable, rude, and impersonal, even unapproachable or "unfindable" when most needed. Then there are those who, exemplary in appearance, are bitter within themselves: against the Church, against their vows, against life. They devote their love to ambition, to money, to secret and illicit pleasures. A true love might regenerate them or preserve them from degenerating. If the autocratic Church intends you to be more democratic, why does she not solicit a poll and judge by the majority of votes? Why cling to a tradition that has become obsolete and alien to the realities of life?

Of course, I am not questioning here the magisterium of the Church nor downgrading the sovereignty of the Supreme Pontiff. I am appealing to them. There is no question of dogma or morals involved here, only a disciplinary measure. I am not advocating laxity on sex and devaluation of the exercise of chastity. I am asking to curb the deviations and abuses of sex on the part of priests outside of marriage. If the concupiscence of these human angels has been stronger than their promise of chastity, then there is a *"remedium concupiscentiae"*—a sacred one—sanctified by Christ and the Church herself. Is marriage a crime?

I leave it to exegetes to give us the scriptural interpretation, and to theologians the doctrinal application, of Apoc. 14:4: "These are they who were not defiled with women: for they are virgins. These follow the Lamb whithersoever he goeth." But I do not believe that if a priest "adheres" to his wife, this makes him "defiled with women," and a soul reprobate by the Lamb. After all "there are many mansions in my Father's house."

I do not wish to upset the mystical and moral balance of values between celibacy and marriage; I am not becoming, as has been suggested, "more contemptuous of consecrated virginity than the ascetics ever were of marriage." I am asking for a balance. To dissuade a priest from practicing chastity would be to chastise virtue; to condemn a priest for embracing marriage is to declare evil what is not such by its nature. To persist with a law which is against nature is like expecting a river to flow contrary to its natural course; it is like trying to swim against the current: it is difficult or even impossible, and sooner or later one has to give in. Christ did not make heroism a general *sine qua non* condition. Besides, His speech is often highly figurative and cannot be taken *ad litteram*, as, for instance, when He wants us to be as perfect as His heavenly Father, or, *à propos*, when He uses a surgical term in regard to those who may want to emulate the eunuchs of the old oriental queenly courts or harems, "for the sake of the kingdom." He did not recommend a mutilation of that kind—although it is true that the Church practiced it up to quite recently (for the sake of the kingdom?) for the singers of the Sistine Chapel. She has now, however, recognized its turpitude and abolished it, and has, in fact, never allowed the ordination of an emasculated man.

It may be that married priests do not belong to the heroic rank of militants, but Jesus did not declare marriage such a crime of desertion as to deserve *ipso facto* dishonorable discharge, court-martial, *de facto* concentration camp, loss of rights *de jure*. I cannot apply to marriage the counsel of St. Francis of Assisi to Brother Leo on being mistreated for the sake of the Lord: "Write, here is perfect joy." There is no perfect joy in anything on this earth. But there is some joy, nevertheless: physical, as in the food which attracts us so that we can take it and enjoy it for our material conservation, and spiritual, as in the love which makes us bear the responsibilities and the pains of life.

The Church has reversed policy before with a good justification. She should remember that her past inexorability often resulted in gross mistakes and extreme cruelties as, for example, with Galileo and Savonarola. The first was a scriptural blunder that infringed on the rights and findings of science; the second was an unjust repression of the frank voice of a religious man publicly deploring and denouncing the corruption and immorality of the official Church.

History is full of fateful episodes in which Church policies and politics played a perplexing role, where it is obvious that a less intransigent attitude and a more conciliatory disposition on her part could have healed the plagues of a contentious Christianity. It is better to sin for excess of mercy than for excess of justice. Whenever the Church has been unable to look at reality with dispassionate eyes, she has demeaned her divine character and her motherly mission of love and reconciliation. A thin coating of a forced doctrinal veneer is no substitute for Christian charity. Now she is trying to be more benevolent, reconciliatory, and realistic in many fields. For this she is admired and loved. Yet in the confrontation with the problem of religious celibacy she is still unrealistic. There is a real possibility of serious schism.

May Christ from above direct for the best the destiny of His mystical spouse on earth, and the fate of His ministers with human spouses, and of those who wish to take one and still remain in the service of God and His Church.

"*Plain Mister Hooven*"

Herbert Hooven

After seven years in the priesthood, HERBERT HOOVEN converted to married life. He had entered the seminary at age fifteen, was ordained to the priesthood in 1959 in the Archdiocese of Brooklyn, fell in love in May, 1966, and married in October of the same year. Before his marriage he spent six years in parish work and one year as a theology instructor at St. Francis College, Brooklyn. He is now employed as director of the Alcoholic Division of the Bronx County Mental Health Society. Mr. and Mrs. Hooven reside in Brooklyn.

Just a few months ago, I was the Reverend Herbert J. Hooven, a respected member of the local community, a fairly popular and successful college teacher of theology, and a middling graduate student at a local Catholic university. As of this writing, I am plain Mister Hooven, fortunate enough to be married to a lovely, understanding woman. Besides this, I am a conundrum, albeit a loved one, to my family, a figure of contention to some other relatives and friends, and, I suppose, a source of consternation to my former superiors.

At some moments the last several weeks seem like a year, so much has changed. Yet in reality, I am—insofar as anyone can properly say—the same person I always was; only the context of my life has changed. It is much too soon for me to assess correctly my feelings during recent days, but I can give the reader a description of some events in my life and my reactions to them in the hope that he may be helped, not only to understand me, but also to grasp something of what it means to have been a priest in my own generation.

In this short, eventful time I have had long moments of comforting self-pity, hours and nights spent in stultifying fear of new responsibility, queasy bursts of self-doubt. I have also had moments of hilarious good humor, enjoyed the comfort and help of understanding friends and family, felt and lived the challenging love of my wife. Perhaps it is only now that I have begun to emerge as an adult human being. In any case, I shall live the remainder of that adulthood as a married priest.

I decided to become a priest at fifteen, mostly because of the impressive example of a particular parish priest. He was, and still is, a model of unselfish service to his fellow men. It was that ideal of service which attracted me. He guided me into the minor seminary and has been a good friend ever since.

Those years of high school and two years of college were happy and productive for me. The course of studies was impressive and, despite a generally poor faculty, occasionally challenging. But looking back on those years now, I quite easily see how completely insulated they were from what was going on in the city. We had practically no contact with other students our own age—of either gender.

To put it simply, I and all my fellows at school were educated as an elite, and every means was used to reinforce that notion. Even the weekly calendar was arranged for this purpose, so that we were, for example, free on Thursdays instead of on Saturdays. In sermons, in classroom lectures, and by indirection, the notion was strongly inculcated that as minor seminarians we had different social responsibilities from those of other boys. Dating was regarded as an indication of lack of vocation and even attending mixed parties was strongly discouraged.

Given the fact that we were being prepared for a celibate life, none of these strictures seemed unreasonable then. At this point, however, I think that the resulting social narrowness—my own and others'—was decidedly unhealthy. To speak only of myself in this matter, it produced in me a distinct uneasiness in the presence of girls and a very strong sense of guilt on those few occasions when I did attend mixed parties.

In fairness, I should point out that apart from a few talks

on the "facts of life"—which seemed ludicrous even then —there was nothing morbid about the faculty's presentation of the ideal of celibacy. Its value was unquestioned, and the school policy was simply the logical consequence.

As one who has gone all through Catholic schools I can attest to the atmosphere of isolation and fear that is generated by the very system itself, despite the protests of some Catholic educators who say this is not so. There is a definite kind of splitting off of Catholic children from other children in the neighborhood. And when you get into the minor seminary, and the major seminary certainly, the isolation is even more pronounced. In the major seminary, there was, for me, the physical isolation of going away into the country, completely separated from everybody else. I was not allowed out without permission, under threat of expulsion. This separation from everyone except fellow students produces a kind of inversion, and out of the convolution emerges the notion of membership in an elite. The isolation which is common to all Catholic school children is reinforced in the minor seminary to such an extent that it establishes a sense of being different: actually *being* different, not just being in a different situation. And at the major seminary level the notion of "elite" is not only reinforced by the rules and regulations and by the setting of the place, but consciously and openly by the faculty: I must be completely different from everyone else; my concerns will never be the concerns of the average man; I am privileged, one of God's favorites. The attitude is deeply ingrained and therefore difficult to cast off. During the last few months, looking for jobs, I caught myself being surprised to find that people were not treating me as a privileged character. At the root of it, I think, is the Catholic notion of grace, that all Catholics are indelibly marked at Baptism with God's special seal of approval and that the priestly vocation is a conclusive sign of the ultimate in God's gifts to man. The seminarian is taught to treasure this jewel of great price and to protect it against all sorts of dangers. Moreover, because Church authority has, in effect, made celibacy *the* necessary precondition for becoming a priest, the prime danger to be guarded against is that of social contacts outside the system, especially with females.

The fear mentality ties right in—it is all of a piece. In my own case it certainly did. Although my parents were not tyrants, they nevertheless maintained a "good Catholic parents'" commitment to the primacy of obedience: whatever Sister says is right, and since I am the parent here, and so forth, whatever I say is right, and if you don't do what Sister says, things are going to happen to you. In the first grade, Sister would reward the "good little boys" with holy pictures. A "good little boy" meant an obedient little boy who did everything that Sister commanded. It was much the same, in one form or another, straight through the seminary. Always the criterion for reward was obedience. One of our teachers at the major seminary used to say, "If you keep the Rule, the Rule keeps you." Which means that if you are obedient, you have no problems. He actually said to us on several occasions: "Chastity would never be a problem if you were obedient."

One of the major problems about seminary education lies in this attitude. There is a long, detailed Rule that must be obeyed, and everything is put in terms of "It is God's will." The bell is a sign of God's will. I listened endlessly to sermons about the bell in the hall being the voice of God. When the bell rang, Almighty God was calling. The idea of obedience was essential. You could be incompetent in your studies, you could be a complete recluse socially (with the people in the seminary), but as long as you obeyed the Rule, you got by. Many times obedience to the Rule was used as a rule-of-thumb. Many of the faculty made it clear that the basis upon which they could judge our qualifications for receiving Orders was obedience: "Since we have so little contact with you, only when you break a rule do you come to our notice." Thus, a student who kept the Rule perfectly could get through the seminary, even though he might be psychotic. To the extent that there was any relationship with the faculty, it was largely master-servant, or disciplinarian-disciplined. After ordination, when I was assigned to serve as a parish priest, the new life seemed so open, so helter-skelter, in contrast to the rigidity of the seminary, that at first I felt free. But very quickly I began to realize that it was the same thing all over again, with only minor variations. I had moved into the next story, but the structure was the same.

My pastor and I came to the parish at the same time; it was his first assignment as a pastor and my first as a curate. He was as nice as he could be in a million different ways; but when it came to dealing with the people in the parish around him he was completely unaware of their needs, and if one tried to explain them to him he would say: "I've been through all that, and you just don't know what you're talking about, and that's that," or "There's no money for that program," and you can't do this and you can't do that, and there was no discussion. It was simply a question of "This is what I say, and therefore because I say it, since I have been chosen to be the pastor of this parish, I have the authority and you don't; you obey me."

The isolation of a priest is not just a question of being unaware of the people around you; it involves the whole concept of the priesthood. Men of my pastor's time and the men who taught me conceived of a priest as the person in the rectory, available twenty-four hours a day—available, but in the rectory, and no place else. So that their idea of the function of a priest was a person who was there to serve if called upon to serve; it was not the idea of going out and getting involved with people and finding out what they

Married Priests & Married Nuns

needed. Given this notion of the priesthood, plus my pastor's notion of authority and obedience, the result was a big nothing. Nothing constructive happened in that parish. I am not blaming him for it; I am at fault myself. I should have resisted more. We were ministering to a "minority group" parish. There is much that could have been done. I blame the system for producing both of us. In the seminary I accepted everything; I took it for granted that this was all correct, and it took me quite a while to get over it.

Talking to others going through pretty much the same thing in other parishes, I began to realize that the parish structure, at least in "minority group" or "underprivileged" areas, just was not a meaningful structure; it had no relation to anything. These are poverty areas. We might have helped, but our hands were tied by the system. After four years and one too many frustrations, I decided to get out of the parish structure and go into teaching. I felt that there I could do something constructive on my own, without having to fight the whole weight of the parish system.

I asked to be assigned to teaching. I didn't ask for it directly, but indirectly, and the answer came back—"No." Finally, I asked enough people, and things happened, and I found myself in another parish where there was some teaching involved. My new pastor was even more isolated and more unaware of what was happening than my first pastor. Like my former parish, this one was in a poverty pocket. One of the curates was doing his heroic best to translate his genuine pastoral concern for the needy all around us into action. But whatever the project, it always carried with it the extra burden of being clever enough to keep the pastor from hearing about it.

It was during this, my second assignment, that I began to think that celibacy was not the best idea in the world. It began that way, and then it got stronger, and I began to think there really was no reason why this should be the law for all priests. It was then that I started to think about going out and mixing socially.

On our days off, several of us who had been colleagues at the seminary would get together to bellyache about the system and talk about how things could be changed positively. Celibacy certainly came up a great deal. Most of us concluded that there really was no organic connection between celibacy and the priesthood. It was just a disciplinary thing, and for that reason could be changed just as easily as the Friday abstinence from meat was changed. Occasionally we would get dates and go out dancing or something like that, but none of us had any kind of real relationship with any of our dates.

I recall that at that time I could not see any possibility of change in the celibacy rule for a long time to come. Therefore it was a touchy subject. You talked about it with your friends, but you did not bring it up under any other circumstances, because it would bring you under immediate suspicion. We all agreed that it was a simple disciplinary matter, but we also agreed that the mentality of the people who make the decisions—the legal decisions—was so fixed that there seemed to be no possibility of change. But events of the past three years indicate that change could come sooner than most of us dared to imagine. There is the impact of so many priests leaving for marriage, and also, I suppose, the idea of change that came with the council. Also, I think it is true generally that the development of the theology of marriage in recent years with increasing emphasis now being placed on the interpersonal relationship between a man and a woman, rather than the traditional view which seemed to imply that a woman was little more than a utilitarian device, has had an effect on priests. I think, for me, this was a longtime problem. Relationships, as I was taught to conceive them, were extremely standoffish things, very formal, very structured, unspontaneous, unemotional. This was insisted upon in the seminary. Naturally you would have friends in the seminary, but one of the great, terrible dangers—like going into town without permission—was to have a particular friend, to be very friendly with some particular person. And the fear of getting involved that way and the fear of having anything like that noticed tended to stultify relationships. We were very careful about getting too involved or too friendly with anyone. This was a problem for me both in the seminary and afterward.

It was not so much thinking about the theology of marriage, but thinking about personal relationships in general and how important they are—thinking about what it means to be a person, that one is not a person except with others—this is what led me into thinking about changing my ideas about celibacy.

My second assignment lasted two years. By this time I was totally fed up with the parish structure; I did not feel that I could be a part of it any more. I was looking for a way out and decided to try again for a full-time teaching spot. At the same time I also decided to see if there was anyone around who thought the same way, besides this small group of friends I had. So I drafted a statement to the bishop and sent it around to a number of priests, asking: "What do you think of this? Is it too far out?"

The statement called for an overhauling of the parish structure and better relationships between curate and pastor, priest and bishop. The responses were mixed: some thought the statement too extreme, too carping in its criticisms; others were in complete accord. I decided to get everybody together, have a meeting, and talk it out. I called approximately twenty priests, and not just people of my own age, but older people, people appointed by the bishop to their jobs. They all showed up and we had a good discussion. A revised statement to the bishop was hammered out. In the meantime, the bishop got wind of it; he was tipped off to a "revolt" going on among the priests. He asked for immediate delivery of the statement. After he read the document he consented to an appointment with two of us to discuss it. Although he had been bishop for eight years, no one could recall his ever answering a request from a priest for an interview. He was gracious, but he had no conception of what we were trying to tell him, none at all. When we had presented our case, he started talking about the council and how wonderful it was and all the funny things that happened to him in Rome. He went on and on—berating the progressive theologians who were "moving Christ around the Church to some hidden place in the building." Finally, he said: "God bless you, young men, you are doing a fine job." But nothing happened. We never really talked. There was no communication. So we left— and I think that was the point when *I* left. It took me about two more years but I think that was the point where I decided, "This is useless. What can you do with these people?"

Several months later I was assigned as a full-time theology instructor at a local Catholic college. I was in residence in a parish without having any duties there. It was an unusual freedom for me; I had no boss any more except in school. There was no pastor deciding what time I was to be at meals and what time I should be in at night. It was a great feeling of liberation. I started to go to graduate school and was dating regularly the same girl. We dated for about five months, but it didn't work out. When I asked her to marry me she consented only on condition that I leave the priesthood at once. She said: "Leave now, then ask me to marry you and I'll say 'yes.'" I insisted on an unqualified "yes" before I left. Her position was that she didn't want to take all of the responsibility for my leaving the priesthood. If I was already out that would be a different matter. I could not accept the distinction, and it soured me on the whole thing.

Not long afterward I met my wife, Louise. A co-worker of Louise's was going steady with another priest whom I knew well. (They are now married.) They arranged for Louise and me to double date with them. This was in May, 1966. By September I had already been steeling myself for five weeks before telling my parents of our decision to marry. It was a painful experience, trying to gauge my parents' reaction—especially my mother's. Having a priest in the family was the end of the rainbow for them. I was genuinely afraid of what it might do to them. Actually there was only a brief emotional scene. They had suspected something for over a year; they were just waiting for it to happen.

We married on October 15. The ceremony was conducted in an apartment by a close friend, a priest (father of two children) who had been married secretly for two years and was then still actively functioning in the ministry. (Not long after our wedding, Church authorities caught up with him and he was "separated from service.") The fact that we were married before a priest raises the thorny theological question: Were we married "in" the Church? I am sure the canonists at the Chancery Office had a grand time with this one.

They finally caught up to us on December 20. In the interval I had continued to function normally, saying Mass, teaching, etc., but at night I went home to my wife. I wanted to remain "in" until June when I would have my master's degree in theology which I hoped would open up some job opportunities. But someone at the Chancery had gotten wind of the affair and confronted the priest who had married us with the evidence. He readily admitted the truth, so I submitted a letter of resignation to the college, packed up, and left. I also wrote to the bishop, but he did not answer my letter.

I immediately began job hunting and was quite surprised at the minimal eyebrow raising that took place at the employment agencies. One interviewer said to me, quite casually: "What is going on with you people? You're the fifth one to come in here in the last few months."

I have associated myself with a growing group of priests and ex-priests who are preparing to petition the American bishops formally to rethink seriously the whole concept of celibacy. Among other things, the group intends to present the bishops with a plan for a pilot program which would experiment with the re-entry of some of us married defectors into the active ministry—as married men—under certain controlled conditions. At this point I am not sure that I personally would be interested. It would depend upon the type of ministry offered. I know I could never return to serve in a parish in the traditional way. There are so many fundamentals involved which cut deeper than the issue of celibacy—about organized religion itself, about community and human relations which, in my judgment, organized religion should properly serve if it is to take on any real meaning in our time, and about the entire juridical structure of the Catholic Church which historically has been more a source of alienation than reconciliation.

I still consider myself an authentic Christian who is a Catholic. This does not depend on ecclesiastical structures, although I am sure there are those who are ready to impugn my orthodoxy. Catholicism's loss of a true sense of communal fellowship is a betrayal of that which identifies authentic Christianity. I can make a very clear distinction between a truly Christian religious community and the typical Catholic parish created by the Latin Scholastic idolatry of legalism. A fellowship of Christians does not need it. It serves no useful purpose.

There is considerable evidence to show that the bishops of Vatican II were somewhat disposed to tackle the celibacy question with open minds. But guarded hopes for an understanding and compassionate treatment of the problem were suddenly shattered by an arbitrary exercise of power by Pope Paul which, in a single stroke, cut off all possibility of fruitful discussion and debate. The bishops quickly knuckled under. But there was at least one redeeming feature of this failure at the top: It helped keep alive the larger question of the need for clarification and refinement of centuries-old notions of the relationship between Pope and Church.

This question has been raised, for example, in the postconciliar writings of Catholic theologian Hans Küng: "In a conflict between the Church and the Pope, the Church—even though She would have the Gospel behind Her—in any case would come out on the shorter end in view of the overpowering might of the Pope and, as has come to pass, be delivered up for decades to popes who are bad and unworthy in every respect. Then nothing remains for the Catholic save to hope for a miracle of the Holy Spirit which, according to the witness of Church history, did not appear at the time needed during the *saecula obscura* of the papacy. The Church Herself supposedly does not possess any legal means by which in an emergency to defend Herself against a bad Pope." (*Structures of the Church:* Nelson.)

Father Küng does not mean to imply that Pope Paul is "bad and unworthy." His purpose is "to lay bare the original structures [of the Church] that have been covered over in the changes wrought by time." He is convinced that "criticism directed against the Catholic Church, which holds that the Church is helplessly surrendered to Popes," is misguided.

One can only hope that events will support his thesis. Resolution of serious juridical and moral questions (*e.g.,* celibacy and contraception) should not be worked out according to the philosophical and theological preconceptions of one man. They are the proper concern of all the Church. The bishops cannot expect to fulfill their mission of service to the faithful unless they are willing to draw upon the experience, wisdom, and resources of the entire Church membership and the larger world community as well. They must learn to make independent judgments; they must be willing and able to express their conscientious opinions without regard for personal risk.

At this writing it appears that the American bishops have thus far relied, without question, on the Pope's thinking in regard to celibacy. But their intransigency will only provoke a more intense prodding from "below." As in the birth-control debate this "pushing up" is progressive. Something has got to give.

Credo Experto
Donald Hayne

DONALD HAYNE, *fifty-nine, was born in Albany, New York. He was educated at the Christian Brothers' Academy in Albany; the Catholic University of America; North American College in Rome; and Mount St. Mary's Seminary, Emmitsburg, Maryland. He also studied psychopathology at Iowa State University. In 1933 he became a priest; nine years later he left the ministry. He married in 1949 and is the father of two children. The marriage ended in divorce on March 30, 1959. He has been Professor of Religion at both Mount St. Mary's College and Iowa State University. For fourteen years he was executive assistant to Cecil B. DeMille, Paramount Studios, in Hollywood. He now lives in Santa Barbara, California. For many years he has devoted much time to counseling and otherwise assisting Catholic priests with special problems arising out of their state in life.*

In his encyclical letter *Sacerdotalis Caelibatus*, dated June 24, 1967, Pope Paul VI definitively settled the juridical aspects of the celibacy question—for a while.

Of course, the Roman Catholic Church will eventually allow its priests to marry. As Father John A. O'Brien has put it, optional celibacy is an idea whose time has come. But ideas are one thing. Institutions are another. The history of ideas in the Roman Catholic Church is a history of institutional time-lag and always belated catching-up. It took us four centuries to catch up with the Protestant reformers in the matter of a vernacular liturgy, for example, and three centuries to catch up with William Penn and Roger Williams in the matter of religious liberty. The time-lag is lessening now, because the progress of ideas, in every field of thought, is faster now than it was in years gone by. The growing consensus on contraception is an example of that: it will probably take us only decades, rather than centuries, to catch up with the position of the Lambeth Conference of 1930 in the matter of contraception. So it will be with other ideas whose time has come, with polygenism, for example, with our necessary rethinking of the whole concept of the *magisterium*, and so on. So it will be with clerical celibacy. The assurance of the first sentence in this paragraph is based quite simply on an objective reading of history.

The same objectivity, however, requires us to recognize that the change to optional celibacy will not come as soon as some have hoped. In the light of *Sacerdotalis Caelibatus,* we cannot reasonably expect the idea of optional celibacy to be institutionally implemented until some time after the beginning of the next pontificate, at the earliest. I do not think we are warranted in prophesying any more precisely than that; but that much seems certain. Juridically, the case for optional celibacy is closed for the foreseeable future by *Sacerdotalis Caelibatus.*

The problem of celibacy remains undiminished, if not aggravated. The discussion of celibacy will therefore continue substantially unabated, until the problem is resolved by the juridical change adumbrated in the preceding paragraphs. The discussion is an inevitable element in the historical process which will culminate in the change to optional celibacy. To recognize that fact is not equivalent to espousing any historical determinism, neither is it disrespectful toward the papal office. We can give to a papal pronouncement even the "religious assent" which the bishops of the United States tell us we should give to *Sacerdotalis Caelibatus,* without being thereby required to blink away evident facts. The continuing discussion of celibacy is one such fact. It is self-evident that the discussion of celibacy remains open. Therefore a book like this, bringing together an assortment of experiences and opinions, varying in their purport and their cogency, but all inspired by a kinship of concern for the well-being of the people of God, is not only a legitimate contribution to that discussion but can be a valuable one. Such, at least, is my hope in taking part in this symposium.

My chief work for some years past has been counseling troubled priests and religious. The problem of celibacy is by no means the only factor troubling the lives of those who have sought my counsel. I am not prepared to say that it is the greatest single factor, but a major and important factor it certainly has been and is.

In speaking of my work I have sometimes felt it necessary to stress that I never attempt to offer anyone ready-
made solutions to anything. As I once put it to some in-
quirers who were pressing me for generalizations, "I don't
want to *make* anyone anything but free—free to make his
or her own mature, conscientious decisions. The process of
attaining that freedom and maturity involves a starkly honest facing and appraisal of one's self—and there I may be
helpful. But once a mature, conscientious decision is freely
made, that is the will of God for that individual, whether I
agree with it or not. Like it or not, it is my duty to help him
achieve it, or else the words I say every day when I don't
forget them, 'Thy will be done,' are utterly phony on my
lips."

It is in that spirit that I address myself here to the problem of celibacy. I have primarily in mind priests of the
Latin rite and those near and dear to them by whatever
kind of bond, for it is with these that the problem of celibacy is most personally acute. For non-clerical religious,
men or women, the vow of chastity may entail similar problems, but their existential situation differs both canonically
and psychologically from that of priests, and at least their
canonical problems are generally more readily soluble than
those of priests under the present discipline. But some of
what I have to say may, I trust, be of some value to the non-
clerical religious also.

Under the discipline prevailing now and for the foreseeable future, a priest to whom celibacy is a personal problem—a priest who wants to marry—has three live options.
Only he can tell, before God and his conscience, which will
be authentic for him. He can opt to remain in the active
priesthood, foregoing the possibility of marriage. He can
apply for a dispensation from celibacy, resigning himself to
abandoning the exercise of his priesthood if the dispensation is granted. Or he can leave the active priesthood with-

out dispensation and marry civilly, thereby, in effect, cutting himself off from his Church. Whether or not a priest choosing the third option incurs excommunication depends upon the applicability of the standard canonical principles—no censure is ever incurred automatically "in the forum of conscience" unless the act involved is subjectively gravely sinful; but, practically speaking, most priests who marry civilly consider themselves cut off from the Sacraments, and I shall not pause over possible exceptions beyond acknowledging their possibility.

Statistics are outside my present purview. In any case, there are few reliable statistics in this whole area. However, there are evidences that, while the majority of priests are still remaining celibate more or less contentedly, both the number of those seeking dispensation and the number of those marrying civilly without dispensation are increasing. Who knows how many more there are, still in the active priesthood, who in the privacy of their own thoughts are contemplating marriage? A sufficient number, surely, to be a matter of concern, of sympathy, and—to speak from my experience of those who have come my way for counsel—of some disquiet.

I had better explain my disquiet. I am not disturbed by the marriage of a priest when that represents an authentic, mature, conscientious decision. I am disturbed when it is a decision taken immaturely, grounded in misinformation and false hopes.

It is heart-rending to read some of the letters I receive from young priests who seem to imagine that marriage will be a panacea. It is neither panacea nor perpetual picnic. Ask any married man or woman. I do not mean to disparage, like a perfect Manichean, the values of married life. That would be, at best, a gross public injustice to the person who shared them with me for a time. But they have their cost, as she might be better able than I to recount. I shall return to her between, if not patently in, these lines.

Some of the agitation for optional celibacy resembles T. S. Eliot's notion of the worst treason: it asks the right thing, but for deplorably inadequate, if not the wrong, reasons. I have had numerous letters from priests who want to marry. Not all those correspondents have seemed to be subordinating their natural and, as I think it, legitimate desire to a diligent seeking of the will of God or to the good of the people whose ordained servants they are.

The personal anguish of the unwilling celibate is in itself reason sufficient to warrant another look at our old law. We are already late in taking that look. But to base our reappraisal of compulsory celibacy on that personal anguish alone is, it seems to me, to miss the point of what law is for, and to miss the point of why compulsory celibacy is outdated. It is not because Father Tom finds it hard to remain chastely celibate. So does his unmarried brother. So does his divorced neighbor down the street. So do his parishioners' sons in Vietnam. Christ promised to make us free; He did not add "and easy."

Neither, I think, is compulsory celibacy to be deemed outdated simply because a growing number of Father Toms are discovering, in life-experience and in a deepened theology, what marriage might mean for their own completion as human beings.

If compulsory celibacy is outdated, it is because it has become a positive handicap to the Church's mission. If I seem at this point to argue, it is argument from experience. I have known priests intimately for nearly fifty years. I have been one, in parish work and college teaching. And, since I have never made a secret of my status, people, Catholic and other, have talked to me about priests more freely perhaps than they talk to the priest in the rectory.

In an earlier age, celibacy had a mystique about it which no doubt had value among an unlettered people who looked up to the priest as a man in every respect their superior. He was not only more learned, more cultured, more traveled, more competent in every field; he was also a man above the base necessities of sex. In this age, the professional celibate is more likely to be looked upon not as something more than a man, but as something less.

It will not do to decry this view simply as another sign of modern decadence. History is the teacher of life. Pope John said: "In the present order of things, Divine Providence is leading us to a new order of human relations . . . directed toward the fulfillment of God's superior and inscrutable designs." Nowhere is this more evident than in the changed relationship of clergy and laity in the Church. Today the priest is respected for his liturgical and sacramental office; and for anything else only insofar as he demonstrates a competence derived from his personal qualities, training, and experience. In the areas of life in which he has no experience, he tends to be more and more disregarded. Who, anymore, considers his pastor the last word in politics, economics, education, literature, art, or manners? And how long will the laity of today continue to regard as an authority on family life the man who is forbidden to have a family?

Professional celibacy is more and more regarded by people outside of the Church as something simply odd or stunted. The people of the Church are groping their way toward a deeper appreciation of conjugal life, seen now not as a concession to the "weak flesh," but as a source of human, and indeed "spiritual," fulfillment. Inevitably this is already altering, in Catholic minds, the image of the professional celibate as a necessarily superior being. He is seen as a man whose ideas of life are founded in a remoteness from life; and this is a man whom the modern world will politely pass by and ignore.

It is for closer love and better service of that world,

which God so loved, that His and the world's priestly servants should be permitted, if they will, to take up the awesome burdens and responsibilities of marriage. If, or rather, when a future pope makes that stroke of the pen which good Pope John declined to make, I believe a substantial minority of priests (I do not now speak of certain types we all know: the selfish bachelor, the latent homosexual, the clerical Miniver Cheevy) will freely choose and adhere to a celibate life because they will see that voluntary celibacy can give a priest a greater measure of independence and freedom to fulfill his prophetic vocation of service than a man has who has given "hostages to fortune."

There was wisdom in Pope John's hesitancy. There should be more discussion of celibacy and marriage as live options for the clergy, and of the values that each may hold for the individual and for the Church, and this discussion should not be, as some have suggested, a clerical preserve. The well-being of the priesthood affects every member of the Church; and here, if anywhere, that public opinion which Pope Pius XII said was so necessary to the Church should be vocally operative. Eventually, seminary instruction and discipline will have to be accommodated accordingly. All this will come; God grant that it will not be too, too late.

Meanwhile, in unknown numbers, they—we—are leaving, and marrying, and learning, almost totally unprepared, what marriage is and is not like. An Anglican friend once quoted one of his seminary teachers to me: "When you go into a parish, you will have no peace unless you do one of two things: announce firmly that you are a celibate, or marry the first girl who proposes to you." An Anglican, with the strong tradition of a married clergy behind him, might conceivably find peace in that latter drastic alternative. Not we Romans, unless by a lucky fluke or special grace of Providence. We—and that includes our future marriageable clergy as well as those in my position, with or without dispensation—are more likely to find the bitter truth in the old adage about marrying in haste. (I did not marry the "first girl," by the way; and my wife did not propose to me.)

The "first girl" is always a glamour girl! She may be forty and dowdy but she is Heloise to our fumbling Abélard. And no wonder. In our thirties or forties or fifties, most of us are adolescent in this area. We may have combed the marriage manuals of Monsignor Thisorthat, written, as likely as not, out of years of experience in the warm, domestic atmosphere of some Chancery Office. We may even know our Oraison or Lepp or Vann by heart; but no theoretic knowledge prepares us for the first experience of human love, the wonder of discovery and response, and the later, inevitable, most natural, most wholesome, but all too often devastating discovery of reality and of love's costs.

I had a shrewd spiritual director in my youth. Whenever I went to him full of romantic notions about being a missionary or a monk, he would point out the difference between listening to the missionary's pulpit eloquence and living with that same man in community. Sometimes, he would draw me vivid verbal pictures of the novices chanting office in choir while the fathers took their naps, for their delicate health, of course. His shrewdness has a wider application. Have we found the reality of marriage or the priesthood what we imagined it in our chronological adolescence? Heloise in curlers and vanishing cream, Heloise periodically irritable or morose, Heloise full-panoplied with all the foibles undiscovered until many mornings after, can be as destructive of illusion as any pastor sitting up there at the head of the table with his mind encased against the intrusion of a new idea and his curates suffering more than he does from the reactions of his abused liver. (I must parenthesize again to say that, while all three had their foibles, my wife happened to be as attractive in curlers as at a cocktail party and the only two pastors I had were men who merited the lifelong respect in which I hold them.)

To cope with the realities of married life we are not only negatively unprepared, as is many a young husband; our seminary training has put a positive premium on immaturity. Who was it that said that "a seminary is a place where men are turned into boys"? When the students of one American seminary "demonstrated" about something or other in 1966, I remarked that if I were a bishop (a fate which kindly Providence has spared me and the Church), I would be peeking out through my lace-curtained window at the demonstration and dancing a little jig of joy that my students showed that much gumption. But we learn early enough in clerical life that, as a rule, the seminarian or the priest who gets along is the one who goes along. His gumption is confined to well-worn grooves. Our intellectual training, purposefully anti-empirical, follows the same pattern. We are taught to think in terms of neat categories, of abstract essences. Is there any group of men fonder than we of those two most abused words in the English language, "is" and "should"? (Perhaps I am speaking here more justly of seminaries and priests of my generation than of newer breeds. There are some fresher breezes blowing through those windows opened by Pope John. But paleo-scholasticism dies hard.)

That philosophical excursus is by no means irrelevant to our topic. The assurance our standard intellectual training gives us as to what we know what is and what should be tends to create in us what I may call an inflexibility of expectation. Persons so conditioned (we priests are not the only ones by any means) often get emotionally upset, sometimes severely, when they find that chunks of reality do not correspond to the verbal definitions which they have equated with reality. How many of the troubled nuns who write to me, for example, are troubled principally because they find that their own sense of identity does not fit that of the taught model. If this "inflexibility of expectation" can give rise to wholly unwarranted guilt feelings, it can also produce, in our relations with others, the psychological effect which Jungians call projection.

Projection—looking for or imagining we see in others the attributes which we consciously think or unconsciously desire should be there—is a universal human device. The human race would have become extinct long since without it, for few young persons would (as one young priest described his own experience to me) "fall gloriously in love" unless part of that glory were the imparted glory in which the lover's projections deck the beloved. But, if projection makes an appetizing *apértif,* it is far from a sustaining, steady diet. It is the withdrawal of projections and the clear-eyed acceptance of reality in their place which are at once source and sign of psychological maturity. How many priests can recall ever having been told that anywhere in their training? We cannot, however, fault our training for not having prepared us specifically for marriage! But, if any priest is contemplating marriage, whether as a present or theoretically future option, he will be well advised to remember that "inflexibility of expection" does not prepare one to cope with those most unpredictable of God's creatures—wives.

Young priests write to me inquisitively about what it is like "out there." I respond that it is an untidy world, not like that known through the seminary manuals which so clearly map everything as it "is" and "should be." Yet every fragment of it, from fairest flower to most bruising stone, is a *vestigium Dei.* One should kneel down before that fact like a little child, as old T. H. Huxley might well have put it. That, I suggest, is the meaning of that tremendous commitment, "for better, for worse": better or worse than I imagine thee now thou surely wilt be; but so, to have and to hold, from this day forward, I take *thee*. Are we ready for that? I was not; and I am not the only one who suffered from my immaturity and unreadiness.

I can repeat, gratefully, here or anywhere, what I have written elsewhere of my marriage:

> It was in marriage that I grew to adulthood, if I have done so at all. It was in marriage and parenthood that I learned, if I have learned at all, the costly steadiness of giving and forgiving, sharing and forbearing, the creative anguish in the cup that will not pass because love holds it steadfast to our lips.
>
> I never knew what it means to call God our Father until I held my own babies, so totally dependent, so utterly trusting, in my arms.
>
> Christian theology has words for all these things. In marriage and parenthood, the words and the things become more real to me than ever before.*

Good schooling. But its tuition costs were not cheap. And I was not the only one who paid them.

The "forgotten man" in much discussion of clerical marriage (or its facsimiles or counterfeits) is the woman. I speak here less of the wife of an active or dispensed priest —there are to my knowledge none of the former of the Latin rite in the United States and as yet too few of the latter to generalize on their experience—than I do of the woman who is or functions more or less as if she were the wife of a priest still canonically bound to celibacy. I call her "man" because what is principally forgotten about her in these discussions is that she is also a human being, with all the "dimensions, senses, affections, passions" of our human kind. She is also a human being redeemed by the same Precious Blood in the priest's chalice. She is often a

* From the author's autobiography, *Batter My Heart* (New York: Alfred A. Knopf, Inc., 1963).

human being caught in a peculiarly tearing anguish which can be known only by one who has experienced it—or caused it. Ecclesiastical officialdom often regards her only as a thing: to be set aside, deserted, abandoned, paid off, got rid of in any possible way within the law, so that the priest is "saved." There are priests who accept that kind of "saving," and of course there are honorable exceptions. A worldly man of honor, faced with the hard necessity of divorce, does all he can to provide for the needs of his wife and children. So there are priests, I know, who long to return to the exercise of their priesthood, but wait for years until they can first provide, economically and emotionally, for the security of lives for which they have taken responsibility. So there are ecclesiastical superiors, I know, who act with understanding and compassion for all the human beings caught up in these often terribly tragic dilemmas. But there are women who trusted us and did not find in us that honor or that grace. Their fate might give a moment's pause to any who contemplate marrying one of us.

But—at best—suppose that we are all, all honorable men. That is not enough. Dr. Robert McAfee Brown has been quoted as saying that, while some of his best friends are priests, he would not want one of them to marry his daughter. Perhaps, as I recall it, he said Jesuits; but no one could accuse Dr. Brown of discrimination. A competent and experienced canonist, voicing his misgivings about some of the pending applications for dispensation from celibacy, wrote to me recently: "Some men would just make lousy husbands." It is not the business of ecclesiastical authority to decide in individual cases, but priests must examine themselves with complete honesty. Being accustomed to think of ourselves as the ambassadors of God to men is no ground for thinking that we are His gift to women. Our male vanity, not to say our clerical arrogance, is tellingly revealed in the assumption, implicit in many of these discussions, that when a pope does pick up that pen and make that stroke, there will be, say, thirty thousand women in the United States ready and waiting to marry us. Has anyone asked *them?* There will be, of course, a sufficient number, armed with the same kind of projections, actuated by the same kind of mixture of motives that impel us toward them—or that impelled us toward the priesthood in the first place. That is part of the human condition; those are elements in every marriage. They are not insuperable obstacles, given an adequate measure of intelligence, understanding, and love on both sides. A woman can indeed be a helpmate to enhance her husband's Christian ministry. But when a young priest writes to me that celibacy is now the chief topic of conversation among the young priests of his acquaintance, I cannot help wondering what proportion of that conversation is devoted to a wife's part in their ministry to others, and what proportion to ministering to their own desires. Those desires are legitimate, I believe. But a faithful priest puts first in his considerations the well-being of other people, and a faithful lover puts first the one he loves. There is no essential incompatibility between the two, if we are adequately prepared.

One day a pope will make that stroke of the pen and—eventually—the Church will experience from it, if it is not too late, a rejuvenating effect. How soon that will come depends precisely on how well prepared we are for it. Let it be a topic of conversation, of scholarly research, of personal testimony, of debate, and of dialogue with those of the other confessions who have a body of experience in this area from which we can learn much. That preparation is essential if the coming change to optional celibacy is not to bring in its train as many problems as it solves.

For the individual priest who contemplates marriage, a similar personal preparation is equally essential. It must go deep. The suggestions explicit and implicit in this chapter

230 Married Priests & Married Nuns

and elsewhere in this book hardly do more than glance over the surface of some of the elements involved in so momentous a decision, if it is to be mature. In my experience, many priests and religious, like many other people, would profit by a stint of professional psychological analysis and counseling. And all of us will profit by unstinting and bravely honest prayer.

I conclude with words not my own, words we have read often to others. I shall probably never hear them read to me. But I copy them here from a borrowed book (for mine has been long lost), hoping that we may read them now, afresh, as if new-minted, newly known, weighing each word and weighing ourselves against each word. He that can take these words, let him take them:

> Dear friends in Christ: . . . You are about to enter into a union which is most sacred and most serious, a union which was established by God himself. By it . . . He enabled man and woman to help each other live as children of God, by sharing a common life under his fatherly care. . . . And so he gave to Christians a new vision of what married life ought to be, a life of self-sacrificing love like his own. . . . We are willing to give in proportion as we love. . . . The rest is in the hands of God.°

° *Collectio Rituum pro Diocesibus Statuum Foederatorum Americae Septentvionalis* (Liturgical Press, Collegeville, Minn.).